FROM
SUPERVISOR

to

SUPER LEADER

HOW TO BREAK FREE FROM STRESS
AND BUILD A THRIVING TEAM
THAT GETS RESULTS

SHANDA K. MILLER

PINE BENCH

PINE BENCH PUBLISHING
Eugene, Oregon

Published by Pine Bench Publishing, Eugene, Oregon
Ordering Information
For additional copies email support@shandakmiller.com
Quantity discounts are available
Credits
Cover Design: Maggie Ziomek, San Francisco, California
Author Photo: Jennifer James-Long
Editing: Qat Wanders and her team at Wandering Words Media
Interior Book Design: Hynek Palatin
Paperback ISBN: 978-1-7337128-5-9
eBook ISBN: 978-1-7337128-9-7
First Edition

DOWNLOAD THE FREE BONUS CONTENT

To say thank you for buying my book, I would like to give you access to the bonus material referred to in this book:

- Leadership Purpose Workbook
- Self-Assessment Worksheet
- Bonus Chapter: Create a Support and Accountability System

Download it now!

https://geni.us/SLbonus

To Kent, for his unwavering love and support,
and for adopting my dreams as his own.

CONTENTS

Author's Note: The Practice of Team Leadership   ix

PART 1: LEAD YOURSELF   1

   Practice 1: Know Yourself   3

   Practice 2: Know Your Why and Work on Purpose   17

   Practice 3: Know Your Roles   33

PART 2: LEAD YOUR TEAM   45

   Practice 4: Build Trust and Strong Relationships   47

   Practice 5: Build Your Team   55

   Practice 6: Delegate Effectively with Clear
   Expectations and Feedback   71

   Practice 7: Coach Your Team to High-Performance   89

PART 3: LEAD YOUR BOSS   101

   Practice 8: Build a Strong Relationship with
   Your Boss   103

   Practice 9: Lead Up   111

Begin Your Team Leadership Practice   121

Acknowledgements   133

References   135

About the Author   143

Review Request   145

Take the Next Step in Your Journey   147

THE PRACTICE OF TEAM LEADERSHIP

I'm glad you found this book. If you're in charge of a team or wish to be a team leader one day, this book is for you.

Maybe you were promoted to a position where you're leading a team for the first time. Maybe you're an entrepreneur who now finds yourself with a team of employees. Or perhaps you're an aspiring supervisor and you want to develop new skills to prepare you for the next level.

Or you're a supervisor who is struggling. You feel you're holding your head above water, and fearful you're not meeting expectations. Perhaps you're concerned your team is not engaged and you're not connecting with them. Or you worry you micromanage too much.

Even worse, maybe you're feeling like a fraud, that you don't have what it takes to lead a team. You realize being an expert in your field doesn't guarantee you have the skills to be a successful team leader.

No matter what your title is, if you are responsible for a group of people working toward a shared goal, you are a team leader.

As a team leader, you juggle a lot of responsibilities. You're responsible for your team and their completion of deliverables and objectives. You need to manage your teams and your own work, and at times you need to manage up.

With all these responsibilities, it's easy to fall into the trap of overwork and overwhelm. It's often also the expectation that team leaders work long hours and take work home with them.

I hear more often from friends and colleagues that work-life balance is important to them. Our culture of instant notifications, to-do lists, and synced calendars have made our lives more hectic than ever. Maybe you realize you are neglecting important areas of your life. You believe there is more to life than long hours and high stress.

I wrote this book to help break the myth that to be a successful team leader you must work long hours. This book will give you the confidence and skills needed to be a successful team leader. This book contains concise and easy-to-read practices you can implement right away.

As a team leader for 20 years, I took numerous trainings and read the best books and articles on the subject of team leadership. I implemented and tested what I learned. In this book, I compiled what I found to be the best team leadership practices.

Like the practices of law and medicine, we practice team leadership. The practices I have compiled in this book will help you build thriving teams that get results within regular work hours.

After I found and implemented the team leadership practices I share in this book, I found myself and my team members functioning as a high-performing team. My team and I:

1. Had more fun and less stress
2. Enjoyed a high level of trust and camaraderie
3. Learned together and grew together
4. Shared failures and successes
5. Worked at a high level of productivity
6. Met our objectives and deliverables on time and on budget
7. Left work on time and didn't take work home

I promise if you follow and implement the nine practices described in this book, you'll be able to build high-performing teams. Teams that consistently meet deliverables and objectives on time and on budget. I also promise you'll be able to leave work on time every day, confident your team is on target and meeting expectations.

Don't be the team leader who falls for the myth that team leadership means being overworked and overwhelmed. Be the team leader who makes it look easy. Be the team leader who invests in continuous growth and development for yourself and your team. Take your professional development into your own hands, and like me, you too can become a successful team leader.

Whether you're a team leader in an office, customer service environment, production floor, or start-up business, you're in for an adventure on your way to becoming a super leader—someone who is successful at leading yourself, your team, and your boss.

Unplug this weekend and read this book. Then Monday morning begin to implement and practice what you've learned.

These practices may not always be easy. But if you implement and practice them, you'll achieve exceptional results, transform your team, and win as a team leader.

Regards,

Shanda K. Miller
December 30, 2018

PART 1

LEAD YOURSELF

KNOW YOURSELF

*"There is always a gap between the self we
think we present and the way others see us."*
– Douglas Stone & Sheila Heen, *Thanks for the Feedback*

LEARN YOUR BLIND SPOTS

Blind spots are things we don't see about ourselves, but others do.

The biggest personal transformations and break-throughs in leadership come from doing the work to know ourselves more. On the other hand, what we don't know about ourselves—our blind spots—can hinder our success.

Early in my career, I didn't know my usual facial expression was blank and caused others to see me as unapproachable. My husband calls this my deadpan face. Before I knew this about myself, I didn't understand the effect it had on others. It was one of my blind spots.

In my early twenties, I began to learn more about myself and to have the self-esteem and confidence to seek feedback. I signed up for a leadership course, and one assignment was to seek specific feedback from the people I worked with and was close to. Here are examples of the feedback questions I asked:

- What do you see are my strengths?
- What do you see are my weaknesses?
- What do you think others say about me when I'm not around?

I saw how the people in my life could be a mirror for me. This mirror allowed me to see myself as others saw me. My deadpan expression was one thing I learned.

When I understood that others saw me as unapproachable was *huge*. Being unapproachable was not my intention. I want to seek connection and acceptance from others.

I saw that my desire did not match my facial expression. Now that I understand this about myself, I am more aware of my expression and try to smile, make eye contact, and acknowledge people. I also tell my friends and colleagues this is my go-to face, and not to make it mean anything.

Learning this blind spot allowed me to see myself in the world and to show up the way I intend.

You too can learn your blind spots. Asking for feedback from others is your mirror to seeing what you can't see. Learning our blind spots can be painful. Don't ask for feedback when you're emotional or vulnerable. It's also best to ask for feedback in doses and specific to one thing at a time.

RECOGNIZE YOUR LIMITING BELIEF

Like blind spots, we can also have a limiting belief about ourselves and our abilities. Often this limiting belief is hidden from us because we are not conscious of it.

We all have some form of the limiting belief "I'm not good enough." This limiting belief can put a ceiling on our success and keep our expectations low.

Often, there is a negative event that happens when we are young children that triggers us to make a decision about who we are. This decision becomes a core belief about ourselves. Then we set out to either prove or disprove this belief.

My core limiting belief showed up as "I'm not smart enough." I found my limiting belief by reflecting on the stories I had about myself. For me, the event occurred in the first grade when my teacher bumped me from a higher reading group to a lower one. To my six-year-old brain, this was devastating. I believed the reason my teacher bumped me to a lower reading level was that I wasn't smart enough.

I carried the belief "I'm not smart enough" with me into early adulthood. As I recognized this limiting belief, I realized I was out to prove that I *was* smart enough. I graduated from college at the age of 22 with a 3.2 GPA.

Even with my early successes, I believed there was a limit to what I could do or be. This belief nagged at me even as I landed my first professional job. It nagged at me throughout graduate school and also popped up while I wrote this book.

Now, each time my limiting belief shows up I can choose not to let it stop me.

You might also have a belief about yourself that limits you. Once you recognize the belief, you can do the work to understand it and identify what incident may have prompted it.

One way to recognize your limiting belief is to listen to your self-talk. Is there a common criticism you have of yourself? Was there an event when you first decided you weren't good enough?

You can have great breakthroughs in your work and life when you can recognize and understand the limiting belief that has been hidden from you. This is because you can now choose to no longer let your limiting belief stop you.

EVALUATE YOUR STRENGTHS AND WEAKNESSES

When we know our strengths, we can leverage them and build upon them. We can also grow and become better leaders when we understand our weaknesses or what's hidden from us. When we work from our strengths and self-knowledge, we can find true success.

According to Peter F. Drucker in *Managing Oneself*, most people get it wrong when they think they understand what their strengths and weaknesses are.

Like our blind spots, the best way to learn our strengths and weaknesses is from feedback.

When we ask for feedback from others, it's important we learn how to receive feedback well. It can be hard for us to receive feedback. We want to learn about ourselves, so we can grow as leaders, but we also want others to accept us as we are. Receiving feedback well is a skill we can learn and one that gets easier the more we practice it. It's like building a muscle. Here are a few tips on how to receive feedback:

- Invite feedback in a way that leaves you in control. Ask for specific feedback. For example, in their book *Thanks for the Feedback*, Stone and Heen suggest asking "What do you see me doing or failing to do, that is getting in my own way?" or "What's one thing I could change that would make a difference to you?"
- Understand the feedback. Have you heard this observation before? Be open and consider the feedback could shine a light on a blind spot. Get a second opinion from someone you trust. Most of

our close friends are afraid of giving us their honest opinion because they want to support us and don't want to hurt our feelings. Choose someone you have a strong relationship with and trust. Tell them you want them to be honest.

- Have the right attitude, be in the right space, and be prepared to receive the feedback. When you read or hear feedback, give yourself time to let it sink in. Don't respond right away. Ask any clarifying questions. Sit with the feedback for a while. You'll be less defensive than if you responded right away. Also, you don't always have to accept the feedback.

- Find out how sensitive you are to feedback. If you're more sensitive, then harsh and direct feedback can be upsetting. If you're not sensitive to feedback, then you'll require the person to be more direct. When you ask for feedback, share which type you are, and ask the person to tailor the feedback.

- Be open-minded to the feedback you've asked for. Show openness through your behavior, the look on your face, and your verbal response. If you show you're open to the feedback, the person is likely to continue to give you honest direct feedback. If you're defensive, they will be less likely to be comfortable giving you additional feedback.

Practice these steps on asking for and receiving feedback. You will soon be on your way to increasing your self-knowledge.

Another advantage of asking for and receiving feedback well is you will gain trust and respect from the people you work with. They will also be more willing to continue to give you feedback, which is key to your growth and development.

If you ask for feedback and find yourself with strong emotions or shame, I encourage you to read *Daring Greatly,* Brené Brown's book on vulnerability. Brown has spent much of her career researching vulnerability. She found that when we have the courage to be vulnerable, it allows us to show up in the world and lead full lives with deeper connections with others.

ARE YOU AN INTROVERT OR EXTROVERT?

Also important for knowing ourselves is to understand if we are an introvert or extrovert. Both introverts and extroverts have their own unique strengths.

The biggest difference between introverts and extroverts relates to stimulation.

Introverts have a lower tolerance for stimulation, such as the noise level or number of people in a room. Introverts do better in low-stimulation environments. For example, after a long day exposed to high stimulation, introverts may want to recharge with a quiet evening at home.

Extroverts get energy from high-stimulus environments and go stir-crazy if they spend too much time alone or in a quiet space.

For introverts, too much stimulation can impact their ability to draw upon short- or long-term memories. This means they can have a difficult time thinking on their feet.

I am now a proud introvert, but I used to see it as a weakness. My inability to think on my feet would frustrate me. Because I struggle with job interviews, I have to prepare for every possible question ahead of time.

One of the best examples of the difference between introverts and extroverts is with public speaking. Susan Cain said public speaking is a high-stimulus activity in her book *Quiet: The Power of Introverts in a World That Can't Stop Talking.* Cain said introverts need to prepare more when they are going to speak in public. Public speaking can include sharing ideas in a team meeting or presenting to a large group.

Another difference between introverts and extroverts is the need for introverts to think alone and extroverts to think out loud.

The key strengths of introverts are their ability to listen well and make observations. Introverts are also good at complex problem-solving. In a team environment, an introvert can help the team strategize, think deeply, and solve problems.

Like being able to think on their feet, the key strengths of extroverts are their ability to socialize and network with others, speak in front of large groups, and take risks.

If you're not sure if you're an introvert or extrovert, take the Myers-Briggs Type Indicator assessment. The Myers-Briggs assessment is the most used assessment for understanding individual differences and how we can better work with others. You can take the full assessment with a certified administrator or online for a fee. Go to http://www.mbtireferralnetwork.org to find a certified administrator in your area. Find the Myers-Briggs online assessment at www.mbtionline.com. Or you can take a similar test for free at www.keirsey.com.

Besides introversion and extroversion, the Myers-Briggs assessment offers insight into three other temperament areas: Sensing or Intuition; Thinking or Feeling; and Judging or Perceiving. There are 16 different temperament types. Keirsey.com is a great resource to learn about your temperament type.

ASSESS YOUR EMOTIONAL INTELLIGENCE

In the quest to know ourselves, we cannot leave out emotional intelligence.

Emotional intelligence is our ability to handle emotions well. It's our ability to identify and monitor emotions, either our own or others', and to use those emotions to guide our thinking and behavior.

People with high emotional intelligence—or EQ—can outperform individuals with a high IQ. We can improve our emotional intelligence, whereas people are often stuck with their IQ after they reach adulthood.

In their book, *Emotional Intelligence 2.0*, Travis Bradberry and Jean Greaves offer tips you can use to improve your emotional intelligence. They organize these tips into four EQ skill areas: self-awareness, self-management, social awareness, and relationship management. Bradberry and Greaves co-founded the consulting business, *TalentSmart, Inc.*, which defines each of the four EQ skill areas:

- "Self-Awareness: Your ability to accurately perceive your emotions and stay aware of them as they happen. This includes keeping on top of how you tend to respond to specific situations and certain people."
- "Self-Management: Your ability to use awareness of your emotions to stay flexible and positively direct your behavior. This means managing your emotional reactions to all situations and people."
- "Social Awareness: Your ability to accurately pick up on emotions in other people and get what is really going on. This often means understanding what other people are thinking and feeling, even if you don't feel the same way."

- "Relationship Management: Your ability to use awareness of your emotions and the emotions of others to manage interactions successfully. Letting emotional awareness guide clear communication and effective handling of conflict."

A few years ago, I took *TalentSmart, Inc.*'s emotional intelligence test. The test showed I did well in the Self-Awareness and Self-Management categories. I had room for improvement in the Social Awareness and Relationship Management categories.

The *TalentSmart, Inc.*'s test showed me the areas where I needed to improve. Two of these areas I needed to improve in were listening for other people's non-verbal cues and spotting the mood in a room. I set out to practice these two skills and used specific strategies listed in *Emotional Intelligence 2.0*.

It takes practice to improve your emotional intelligence. As team leaders, we have plenty of opportunities to practice, whether we're working one-on-one or with our team. To find out your emotional intelligence score and areas to improve, take the assessment at talentsmart.com for a modest fee.

FURTHER LEARNING

Daring Greatly: How the Courage to Be Vulnerable Transforms the Way We Live, Love, Parent, and Lead by Brené Brown, Ph.D., LMSW

Emotional Intelligence 2.0 by Travis Bradberry and Jean Greaves

Quiet: The Power of Introverts in a World That Can't Stop Talking by Susan Cain

KEY TAKEAWAYS

- Learn your blind spots so you can show up for others how you intend to.
- Recognize your limiting belief so you can choose not to let it stop you.
- Know your strengths so you can build on them; understand your weaknesses so you can improve.
- Understand your preference toward introversion or extroversion so you can honor the related strengths and challenges.
- Assess your emotional intelligence so you can strengthen your self-awareness, self-management, social awareness, and relationship management.

COMING UP IN PRACTICE 2: KNOW YOUR WHY AND WORK ON PURPOSE

When we know our why—our purpose—our work will be more fulfilling. As team leaders, when we know our purpose and lead from that purpose, we will create more meaning, fulfillment, and job satisfaction for our team members.

The next chapter walks you through the importance of having a leadership purpose. It also shows how important it is to bring purpose to the management of your time. You will learn strategies for working on purpose to achieve exceptional results.

KNOW YOUR WHY AND WORK ON PURPOSE

"If your actions create a legacy that inspires others to dream more, learn more, do more and become more, then you are an excellent leader."
– Dolly Parton

LEAD WITH PURPOSE

Hospital cleaning staff can teach us a lot about purpose. Researchers found they fell into two distinct groups.

The first group of workers saw their work as a thankless job of cleaning up after coworkers and patients. This first group didn't find their jobs enjoyable or meaningful.

The second group of workers saw themselves not just as cleaners, but as having a caretaking role as part of the overall healing process. This second group had purpose and found their work to be meaningful. The workers who saw a greater purpose in their work also changed how they performed their jobs. For example, they took time to visit with patients who didn't receive a lot of visitors.

Our work will be more fulfilling when we have a purpose, or what Simon Sinek calls our why. When we believe our work contributes to an important cause, we have more job satisfaction.

As team leaders, knowing our purpose and leading from that purpose will create more meaning, fulfillment, and job satisfaction for our team members. Simon Sinek talks about this in his books *Start with Why* and *Find Your Why*. According to Sinek, you will motivate and inspire people when what you're passionate about means something to them and becomes personal for them. When people are inspired, they enjoy their work more. They are also more productive and creative.

Purpose is what will distinguish you as a team leader versus just a supervisor. If you don't have your why, your purpose, or whatever gets you out of bed in the morning, you won't have the ability to inspire your team, nor anywhere to lead them. Your team will want to be a part of what you do when they believe what you believe. "People don't buy what you do, people buy why you do it," said Simon Sinek. To lead your team well, lead with purpose.

HOW TO FIND YOUR LEADERSHIP PURPOSE

Our leadership purpose defines us, and it is reflected in how we show up for our team. It's not limited by our title or our team's objective. Our why should be specific and personal. It should light us up and inspire us. Our leadership purpose must also reflect our values.

To find your why and create your leadership purpose statement, take time to reflect. Find a place free from distractions and follow the steps below. You can also download the Leadership Purpose Workbook.

https://geni.us/SLbonus

1. Identify your top five core values.

- Brainstorm a list of values, and list as many as you can.
- Shorten your list of values to your top ten; if you find it hard to narrow the list down to ten, rank them by importance and eliminate values that are similar.
- Narrow your top ten values down to your top five core values; pick the values that speak to your heart and that you could not do without.
- Write your top five core values; identifying your five *core* values will help you understand and prioritize what's most important to you.

2. Create a purpose statement and align it with your five core values.

- Reflect on these questions:

  What most inspires me?
  What do I want to be remembered for?
  How do I want to make a difference in the world?
  What do I do and why do I do it?

- Brainstorm different purpose statements using your core values and answers to the questions above.
- As you draft your purpose statement, make sure it is in the present tense, positive, and action-oriented. Make sure your purpose statement is as concise as possible and easy to remember.
- Write your final leadership purpose statement.
- Post your purpose where you can see it every day.

PURPOSEFUL TIME MANAGEMENT

John works for a software development company and leads a team of coders. At 8:00 Monday morning, John walked into his office, turned on his computer, and checked his email.

By the end of the day, John needed to finish reviewing his team's new software update. But it was Monday, and he would feel better if he checked email first. He spent the first 90 minutes processing his email. He skimmed a couple email newsletters, filled out a training survey, and followed up on administrative requests.

Next, John noticed his mail and other paperwork was stacking up on his desk, so he processed and organized it.

At 10:00, John thought, *I'd better get to that review work.* He took a few minutes to get back into the flow. He had to remember where he left off on Friday. Then at 10:30, one of his team members popped in to ask a technical coding question. This turned into a problem-solving session that lasted until after 11:00. It took John another few minutes to get back into the flow of his review, and soon it was noon. John had been at work for four hours and had only accomplished an hour of focused work.

Can you relate to this story? I know I've had days like this.

John knew what his priorities and goals were. Yet he failed to block out uninterrupted, focused work time and to get started first thing in the morning.

To be a successful team leader, you must plan, control, and manage your work time with purpose and diligence.

Like the members of your team, you must have high expectations for your own productivity and results.

Time management has gotten a bad rap, and for good reason. Most time management strategies focus on getting a lot done, but don't emphasize getting the *right* things done. Our productivity may not be in line with our team's goals. Our organization's culture and norms also may not support proven time management strategies.

The time management principles and strategies provided in this chapter will help you maximize your time in order to get the important things done. They will not help you jam more stuff in your day.

THE PARETO PRINCIPLE

In our work, we tend to spend a small amount of time on the things that produce the biggest results for us. This is the Pareto Principle at work, also called the 80/20 Rule. The Pareto Principle states that for many events, about 20% of the causes create 80% of the effects.

Pareto, an Italian economist, found inequality in income distribution. Twenty percent of the people owned 80% of the land. Others have applied the Pareto Principle to other things, like computer errors. Some have observed that 20% of a software's defects cause 80% of the problems. For business, often 80% of sales revenue comes from 20% of a business's clients.

Others have also applied the Pareto Principle to productivity. It's believed of all an average worker does in an average work day, only 20% matters, and this 20% produces 80% of the results. Therefore, this principle tells us we should focus most of our efforts on the few things that get us the results.

THE POWER OF UNINTERRUPTED, FOCUSED WORK

The days of bragging about our multi-tasking abilities are over. Multi-tasking does not make us more productive. It reduces productivity. It also reduces focus and concentration, which results in needing more time to get things done, not less.

Multi-tasking doesn't work, because what we're actually doing is switch-tasking. Every time we switch tasks, it takes time to re-orient to the new task.

We all have focused work that needs to get done. Yet, just as John experienced in the story above, we rarely create the right environment for getting our focused work done in the most efficient way.

When we begin a task that requires focus, like writing a progress report, it takes us a while to get into the flow. We need to remember our objectives and where we left off.

If we're able to work on the report uninterrupted for four hours straight, we're more likely to get the report done in that time.

The typical work environment does not support large chunks of uninterrupted work. We often start and stop focused work throughout the day. We are interrupted by email notifications, phone calls, and people stopping by our desks. After each interruption, we need a few minutes to remember where we left off and another few minutes to get back into the flow.

STRATEGIES FOR WORKING ON PURPOSE TO ACHIEVE EXCEPTIONAL RESULTS

1. Be clear on your goals and priorities

Get clear on your team's goals and objectives and get clear on your priorities. Every day, decide what is the most important thing you need to work on. Ask yourself:

- What's my biggest goal right now?
- What deliverables or work products relate to that goal?

If you have a specific project you're working on with planned milestones and deadlines, your priority is focusing on and doing the work necessary to achieve the next milestone of the project.

2. Be a planner

After you identify your priorities, plan out your days and weeks. On your calendar, block out uninterrupted, focused time to spend on those priorities.

Start your week with a to-do list that includes what has to get done and in what order of priority. As you attend team meetings and take on more assignments, add those to your to-do list and designate the priority. Your to-do list may include other important yet lower-priority items you can do only if you have time.

Every day, make time for planning. Update your to-do list and look at your calendar to see what meetings you may need to prepare for. When you take time to plan, the rest of your time will be more efficient and effective and you're more likely to work on things that matter.

3. Schedule blocks of time for focused and uninterrupted work

Every day, schedule blocks of uninterrupted time on your calendar. In their book, *The One Thing,* Gary Keller and Jay Papasan recommend a four-hour block of focused, uninterrupted time every day. If four hours is not doable, then schedule two two-hour blocks.

If you have flexibility, schedule these blocks of time during the part of the day when you are most productive. Most people are most productive first thing in the morning. Focused work takes mental energy and most of us are more alert in the morning.

Next, you need to protect your blocks of focused time. Protect these blocks of time just as you would protect an hour meeting with your boss. You may need to set expectations for your team members and your boss, and share how important this time is for you. Help create a culture in your organization where it's the norm for everyone to schedule focused work time. Create this culture with your team first and get buy-in from your boss.

4. Focus on one thing at a time

During your blocks of focused uninterrupted time, work on *one* thing at a time. Pick your biggest priority or the deliverable due first.

When we work on one thing at a time, we get better results. We can also enter a state of flow when we focus on one thing. Being in flow allows us to be more productive and have a satisfying experience.

5. Do your most important tasks first

Like focusing on the right things, it's critical you do your most important tasks first. Most important tasks are those tasks that get you closer to completing a work product or other deliverable.

Instead of working on our important and urgent tasks first, like John, it's easy for us to tackle the little and simple tasks first.

Our most important tasks are also the most difficult and take the most mental energy. These may also be the tasks we least like to do. Thus, we should do the difficult and least fun things first so we have the energy and time to complete them. Doing the hard things first also gives us a sense of accomplishment and momentum for the rest of our day.

Other writers claim Mark Twain said, "If it's your job to eat a frog, it's best to do it first thing in the morning. And if it's your job to eat two frogs, it's best to eat the biggest one first."

We will make the most of our time and achieve our goals if we focus on the things that matter.

6. Let go of the less important

The items on our to-do-list fall into four camps: important and urgent; important but not urgent; unimportant and urgent; or unimportant and not urgent. When we focus on the important and urgent tasks first, the three other types of tasks can accumulate. Keller and Papasan write about the importance of living with chaos. Living with chaos is necessary to be able to focus on our priorities and achieve great results.

For the tasks not aligned with your top goals and priorities, you can batch them. For example, batch together administrative tasks, errands, phone calls, and emails.

When you don't know what to do with the things you don't have time for, follow the four Ds as defined by Julie Morgenstern in her book, *Never Check E-mail in the Morning*:

- **Delete:** *To decide if you can delete a task from your to-do list, ask yourself,* What's the worst that will happen if you don't complete this task? *Also,* Does this task move me forward in achieving my goals? *If not, let it go.*
- **Delegate:** *For each task, ask yourself,* Can I give this to someone else to do? *Or,* Can I delegate this task to a team member or to an administrative support person?
- **Delay:** There may be tasks that are important, but there is no deadline or immediate need to get them done today. Ask yourself, *Can I put this task off?*
- **Diminish:** Similar to delaying a task, perhaps you can reduce the scope of a task. Ask yourself, *What's the minimum needed for this task?* Or, *Is there a shortcut to getting the task done faster?*

7. Use meetings sparingly and on purpose

When you schedule a meeting, make sure it has a clear purpose and a clear outcome. For example, is the purpose of the meeting to brainstorm and share ideas, problem-solve an issue, or make a decision?

You should not use meetings only for the purpose of sharing information. Most people can read twice as fast as you can speak the same information. Thus, put any information you want to share in writing and send it to attendees well before the meeting. Also, tell attendees you expect them to read the information before the meeting. If attendees show up at the meeting and did not read the information, bring extra copies and give them five minutes to read it before you start the meeting.

8. Know when to recharge and practice self-care

Being a team leader can be demanding and requires staying fresh. To stay fresh, it's important to take time to recharge and keep your physical and mental health in shape. The key to staying sharp and energized is to honor when you need a break, extended downtime, or a vacation. In his book, *The 7 Habits of Highly Effective People*, Stephen R. Covey calls this "Taking time to sharpen the saw."

Here are a few important practices for keeping your saw sharp:

- Take short breaks throughout the day and take a lunch break.
- Don't work over 40 hours a week and leave your nights and weekends to personal time.
- Take week-long vacations at least twice a year.
- Find your ideal number of hours of sleep, get those hours, and maintain the same sleep schedule every day of the week.

- Eat a healthy breakfast and lunch to fuel your workday and keep your energy up.
- Keep your body strong and increase your energy by strength-training at least three days a week and getting the equivalent of 10,000 steps a day.

As you practice these, pay attention to what works best for you. Reflect on your productivity and effectiveness after you implement these practices. Notice when you don't make time for a specific practice, and how it impacts your energy levels. When we don't take care of our bodies, this impacts our energy and productivity.

I recommend you don't work over 40 hours a week because research has found more hours at work doesn't lead to more productivity. In fact, studies have found that overwork can lead to less productivity because overwork contributes to higher levels of stress, impaired sleep, and other health problems. Whereas, taking nights and weekends off will make you more productive while you're at work, and you're more likely to work on the things that matter and make fewer mistakes.

Keller and Papasan make this point well, "The people who achieve extraordinary results don't achieve them by working more hours. They achieve them by getting more done in the hours they work."

FURTHER LEARNING

Never Check E-mail in the Morning: And Other Unexpected Strategies for Making Your Work Life Work by Julie Morgenstern

Start with Why: How Great Leaders Inspire Everyone to Take Action by Simon Sinek

The One Thing: The Surprisingly Simple Truth Behind Extraordinary Results by Gary Keller and Jay Papasan

KEY TAKEAWAYS

- When you make your work about something bigger, you'll find greater satisfaction and joy at work.
- Having a leadership purpose will help you engage, inspire, and lead your team to greatness.
- Bring purpose to managing your time and block out focused uninterrupted work time to work on your top priorities.
- Get more done during your scheduled work time so you can achieve exceptional results and leave work on time.

COMING UP IN PRACTICE 3: KNOW YOUR ROLES

Team leaders have different roles than staff members and require different skills. The next chapter introduces you to a team leader's key roles and practices to avoid, such as micromanaging and exerting too much control.

KNOW YOUR ROLES

"Whatever you are, be a good one."
– William Makepeace Thackeray

THE PROMOTION

Mary was Managing Partner in a medium-size accounting firm. Her best team leader retired, and she needed to fill his position. The position was in the Bookkeeping Division, the firm's best performing team with high client satisfaction. Mary's most obvious choice was Chris, the team's most productive accountant.

"I'm honored you've chosen me for this promotion," said Chris. "I will work hard to keep this division the best."

"I'm sure you'll do great!" said Mary.

During her first week as team lead, Chris met with her staff and re-stated her commitment to keeping the division the best. Chris met with Phil, who transferred from the Tax Division to fill her vacated position. Phil was the Tax Division's best employee. She told Phil she would slowly transition her accounts to him. She didn't want to let go of all of them yet.

Things seemed to be going fine, but Chris wanted to make sure the team was performing at its best, so she walked around the office to check on her staff. She noticed each person used a different format for their client reports. In the past year, Chris included additional narrative in her reports to help her clients understand the numbers better.

Chris thought, *What if we increased productivity by using the same report format and increased client satisfaction by having everyone add additional narrative to the reports?*

Chris scheduled a staff meeting and shared the new expectations. She also asked staff to send their reports to her for review before sending them to the client. She thought if she had more control she could guarantee quality and client satisfaction.

Chris's days filled up, but she liked keeping busy, so she didn't mind. Her staff stopped by with questions about the new report narrative.

One staff person said, "I'm not sure I've got this narrative right. Will you look at this report and tell me if I'm meeting your expectations?"

"Yes, I'll take a look and give you my feedback," said Chris.

As she looked over the report, she noticed needed changes. She thought, *It's just as fast if I make these changes myself.* So she did, and emailed the finished report back.

As the weeks went by, Chris became overwhelmed. Her days were full of reviewing and editing client reports and preparing her own client reports. She also experienced many interruptions from staff asking her questions.

Chris came to work earlier to get more done, but it wasn't enough. She was also leaving the office later and later. Being a team leader was a lot harder than she thought. She was working long hours and missing her family.

One morning, Chris received a call from one of the division's clients who asked where his report was. It was late. Chris said she would send it to him by the end of the day. Susan, the accountant assigned to the client, was out sick.

Just my luck, thought Chris. Chris found the client file, and she took all day to finish the report and send it off to the client.

A month after Chris's promotion, the division's performance report was due. While Chris analyzed the performance numbers, she cringed. For each performance category, her division was below expectations. Chris also knew client satisfaction had slipped based on all the client calls she'd been fielding.

The next morning, Phil stopped by Chris's office and asked if he could talk to her.

"Good morning, Phil," said Chris. "How's your transition from the Tax Division going?"

"That's why I'm here to see you," said Phil, "I've decided to transfer back. I've been unhappy here, and it's not just me. When I first transferred, it seemed like everyone had smiles on their faces and they were busy working in their cubicles, but now people seem not to care as much and don't seem motivated. I've talked with others on the team, and they do not feel trusted or supported."

Later that day, Chris walked into Mary's office with her head hung low and a pained look on her face.

"Is everything okay, Chris?" asked Mary.

"No, I'm a total failure," said Chris, as she handed Mary both the performance report and Phil's transfer request. "I realize that even though I performed well as a staff accountant, I'm not prepared to be a team leader. Can we talk about my role and what I need to do to be successful?"

Does this story sound familiar? Have you seen this story play out in your organization? Being a team leader is a different role from a staff member and requires different skills.

A TEAM LEADER'S ROLE DOES NOT INCLUDE MICROMANAGEMENT

A team leader who lacks team leadership skills often defaults to what they know best, doing the work, or having the work done the way they would do it. Another word for this is *micromanaging*.

Most employees run as fast as they can from micromanagers. That's what I did. Early in my career, I worked for a non-profit that had a cause I was passionate about. After six months on the job, I realized my boss was a micromanager whom I allowed to dampen that passion. I pursued a new job.

You can have skilled and competent employees, but give them a micromanager and they will turn into *zombies*. Okay, not that dramatic, but they will become disengaged and unhappy. If you need more convincing, here's a list of additional impacts to staff:

- Fear of disappointing
- Low self-confidence
- Reduced productivity
- Less creativity
- Lack of motivation
- Increased absenteeism
- Resentment

Now you know not to micromanage, but what do you do instead? See eight key team leader roles defined below.

KEY TEAM LEADER ROLES

As team leaders, it's important we learn what our many roles are. Our most important role is to define the team's objectives and guide the team through the process of meeting those objectives. Another key role is to help grow and develop our team members. This chapter introduces the key roles of a team leader. Part II dives deeper into these roles.

1. Engage and inspire

In *Practice 2: Know Your Why and Work on Purpose*, you learned that when team leaders have a purpose, it can inspire themselves and their team. A team leader also facilitates the creation of a shared team vision and shared goals. When team members find personal meaning in your purpose and the team's shared vision, they are more likely to be engaged, motivated, and committed to the team's objectives. Team members are also likely to be more productive and creative.

2. Create a road map

Another role as a team leader is to create a road map for the team. First, it's important to get clear on the team's objectives and then develop a strategic process for getting the team there.

For any strategic process or plan, you'll want to seek buy-in from your team. Share the plan with the team and get their feedback. Revise the plan until each team member can agree and own it. This plan will be the map and guide for how your team will meet its objectives.

3. Be the project manager

A project manager plans and executes a project so it meets objectives and is delivered on time and on budget. If your work is project-based, it's important that you learn and take on the role of project manager.

Project manager responsibilities include developing the project plan. A project plan includes the following components:

- Budget
- Resources
- Scope
- Timeline and milestones
- Roles and responsibilities
- Communication plan
- Risk assessment and mitigation plan
- Work breakdown structure

It is important to share the project plan with the team and get input from them.

The project manager is also responsible for tracking project progress and making sure the team is meeting milestones and deliverables. The project manager communicates project progress to management and works with the team to solve issues.

4. Delegate the work

Another role is to delegate the work. New team leaders tend to struggle with delegation. The key to being an effective delegator is to assign large chunks of work instead of individual tasks. For example, it's better to assign an entire section of a report. This larger assignment should also include the research and any other work needed for writing that report section. This doesn't mean the person can't collaborate with other team members on the analysis or research. When we assign larger chunks of work, this allows staff to have ownership over that work.

It's also important you make sure the team member is clear on the expected outcome of the assignment. Include your expectations for quality and the deadline. If the team member has questions about how to do the work, give them coaching, training, or additional support as needed.

5. Develop staff

One of the most rewarding roles is to grow and develop staff. Work one-on-one with your staff to identify their professional goals and the resources, training, and experience that will move them toward their goals. Refer them to books, training, and other resources. Encourage them to seek other learning opportunities. For their goals that are aligned with the team's objectives, give the person opportunities to gain the experience they need to reach those goals.

6. Be the coach

Like a sports coach, the team leader's role is to coach people to help them be their best and improve. Also like a coach, a team leader can help team members discover their strengths and where they can best contribute to the team. The role of a coach is also to instill confidence and to be a positive force by providing positive feedback on an ongoing basis.

Coaching can and should happen often. Timely coaching allows your staff to make any corrections and improvements right away. Otherwise, staff could create bad habits or become discouraged if you give them coaching too far down the road.

7. Connect and communicate

Another team leader role is to facilitate communication among team members, between different teams, and between the team and management. The team leader also encourages relationship building among team members.

The team leader relays communications to the team, including management expectations. Team leaders also inform management on how the team is doing and update them on team progress in meeting goals and objectives.

8. Facilitate team building and open-minded discussions

A team leader facilitates team formation and team building. This includes creating team norms and agreements for how the team will work toward shared objectives and goals.

A team leader also fosters open-minded communication and discussions. A team leader empowers their team to identify problems and collaborate to solve them.

Open-minded discussions require the team leader to create a culture where team members are free to share their thoughts and opinions. A team that practices open-minded discussions is a more integrated team, and members are more likely to feel good about the process, the decisions, and their team members.

FURTHER LEARNING

Great Teams: 16 Things High-Performing Organizations Do Differently by Don Yaeger

Project Management for the Unofficial Project Manager: A FranklinCovey Title by Kory Kogon, Suzette Blakemore, and James Wood

KEY TAKEAWAYS

- As a team leader, it's important to understand what your many roles are.
- Your role as team leader differs from the role of a staff member and requires different skills.
- Beware of the traps of micromanagement and too much control.
- An important role you have as team leader is to define the team's objectives and guide the team through the process of meeting those objectives.
- Another key role is to grow and develop each team member.

COMING UP IN PART II: LEAD YOUR TEAM

Part II is the core of this book. It begins with Practice 4, which focuses on creating strong relationships and building trust with each member of your team. Building one-on-one relationships is the foundation for creating a high-performing team. Taking the time to nurture those relationships makes work more enjoyable and enables you and your team members to bring your whole selves to work. When our work relationships are strong and trusting, we can work together and communicate better.

PART 2

LEAD YOUR TEAM

BUILD TRUST AND STRONG RELATIONSHIPS

"When the trust account is high,
communication is easy, instant, and effective."
– Stephen R. Covey, *The 7 Habits*
of Highly Effective People

RELATIONSHIPS ARE THE FOUNDATION FOR SUCCESSFUL TEAM LEADERSHIP

Imagine if you have a new person assigned to your team and you make no attempt to create a relationship with that person. How do you think it would go the first time you gave him feedback or had to address a performance issue?

That's what happened to Ann, the owner of Ann's Meat Pie Company. Ann started her meat pie business with a food cart and one employee. Over time, Ann's pies became more popular and in addition to her food cart sales, she sold them at local restaurants, grocery stores, and special events. It wasn't long before Ann went from one employee to four.

One of Ann's new employees was Mark. He was hired to fill orders and deliver them around town. Ann hired Mark on the spot and put him to work right away. Since Mark was out making deliveries most of the time, Ann didn't interact with him very often and didn't make time to get to know him.

A month after Mark was hired, Ann noticed issues with his record keeping. For example, a few of the order receipts were illegible or missing customer signatures.

As Ann prepared to give Mark feedback, she realized she didn't really know him and was nervous and uncomfortable approaching him to talk about the order receipts. She also figured it would not be a comfortable conversation for Mark, either. Ann thought, *It's well past time I made an effort to get to know Mark*, and she made a point to take him out to lunch in the next couple days.

Building relationships is a hot topic in business and government. That is because the quality of our relationships is critical to everything we do and is the foundation for our success.

We interact with our team members, managers, and clients every day. If we put the time into building and tending those relationships, our ability to communicate, work together, and learn together will improve.

The key to creating strong relationships and developing trust is to be intentional, and to make relationship building one of your top priorities.

BUILDING THE RELATIONSHIP

Building a relationship and trust with each team member does not have to happen overnight. Think of each relationship as a long-term investment that begins with building the relationship and continues with ongoing nurturing. When you first work with someone new, meet with them one-on-one at least once a week.

The best way to get to know someone is to ask them to share their life story. Ask them where they were born and raised. Have them share important meaningful events or milestones in their life. Be curious. While they share their story, listen and ask open-ended questions.

After they have shared their story, it's important you also share yours.

In the early weeks of the relationship, also learn each team member's strengths and aspirations. Ask them what their goals are and where they want to be in five years. While your team member is sharing, it's important you suspend judgment, show empathy, and focus on listening.

When you understand your team member's skills, styles, and aspirations, you will connect with them better and get the most out of your interactions.

Also share your strengths, goals, and aspirations. As you learn more about yourself from the strategies in Practice 1, share what you're learning with your team members. Be open, honest, and vulnerable. Share your blind spots, limiting belief, strengths, and the areas you are working to improve. Also, share the leadership purpose you developed in Practice 2. When you share in an open and honest way, it will create the space for them to be open and share with you.

STRENGTHENING THE RELATIONSHIP

As the relationship and trust builds, you can continue meeting once a week or switch to meeting twice a month or once a month.

After you build rapport and trust with each team member, seek specific feedback from the person on how they think you're doing as the team leader. Show you can receive feedback well by listening and asking follow-up questions. Don't be defensive or on guard. If your team member sees you accept feedback well, they will trust you enough to continue giving you feedback.

In *Thanks for the Feedback*, Douglas Stone and Sheila Heen said, "People who are willing to look at themselves are just easier to work with and to live with." If you ask for and receive feedback well, this will be valuable to you and your professional growth. This also can create a more open relationship between you and your team members and creates the space for them to be open and ask you for feedback.

When you and your team members share feedback, this can strengthen the relationship and create the space to learn together when things arise.

MAINTAINING A STRONG RELATIONSHIP

Once you've built the relationship, keep it strong by meeting one-on-one at least once a month. Over time, as the relationship continues to strengthen and grow, you'll have greater confidence in the relationship, greater understanding, and deeper trust. You'll be able to rely on and make requests of each other.

This phase of the relationship also allows for personal growth. You both see the relationship as positive, and you both have greater engagement and commitment to the relationship. The relationship will also be energizing.

EVERYDAY RELATIONSHIP NURTURING

Besides your regular one-on-one meetings with each team member, go out of your way every day to acknowledge each person by greeting them by name and asking how they're doing. Ask them questions about their life outside of work.

A team leader who is a peer of mine goes out of his way every morning to greet his staff and ask how they're doing. One of his team members told me everyone appreciates that daily gesture. Julie Morgenstern, author of *Never Check E-mail in the Morning*, said it well when she stated, "How we treasure (and admire) the people who acknowledge us."

Be sure to acknowledge your team members daily and make yourself available to them. You never know if they will need extra support from you today.

FURTHER LEARNING

Applied Empathy: The New Language of Leadership by Michael Ventura

The 7 Habits of Highly Effective People: Powerful Lessons in Personal Change by Stephen R. Covey

KEY TAKEAWAYS

- Building one-on-one relationships is the foundation for being a super leader.
- Make relationship building a priority and take the time to nurture the relationship with each of your team members.
- Get to know and understand each of your team members well and show you care about them.

- When you bring your whole self to your relationships and allow yourself to be vulnerable, you will foster trust and a true human connection with the other person.
- Having great relationships also makes work more enjoyable and communication easier.

COMING UP IN PRACTICE 5: BUILD YOUR TEAM

Creating a team that works well together, solves problems, and makes decisions requires implementing strategic team building methods. In the next chapter, you will learn how a team becomes a team. You will learn how to build trust and relationships among the team, and how to create a safe and positive culture.

BUILD YOUR TEAM

"There is a strong sense of understanding, appreciation, shared responsibility, and trust that unites and motivates the team to work together."
– Don Yaeger, *Great Teams*

HOW A TEAM BECOMES A TEAM

Often when we think of teams, we think of sports teams. How a sports team becomes a team is not much different from how your team can become one.

First, it's important for team members to share a common vision or goal. As I write this chapter, the 2018 World Series between the Dodgers and the Red Sox is underway. Most likely, members of both these teams have a shared vision of winning the World Series.

Second, it's important that team members know each other, trust each other, and feel accepted and supported by each other. The more team members know each other, the more they enjoy each other. They're also more likely to understand each other's goals and to encourage them. Trust and camaraderie are also important for a high level of cooperation and coordination. People who have a high rapport with their team members are also more likely to share responsibility and commit to doing what needs to be done.

Third, most sports teams bond by sharing a team name, logo, and uniform. Sports teams can also bond in other ways. You may have noticed that baseball teams have players with long beards. I imagine sometime during the season, a player decided to stop shaving, and soon other team members are also growing beards. How bonding happens for your team will depend on what your team comes up with.

Fourth, it's important for the team to have a culture where team members feel safe to express their own views. A culture that fosters empathy and listening to understand allows for open-minded discussions. The team needs to have open-minded discussions to best work together, solve problems, and make decisions.

ACCELERATE TEAM FORMATION

Bruce Tuckman was a research psychologist and professor at Ohio State University. Tuckman is most known for his stages of group development: Forming, Storming, Norming, and Performing. Researchers have since built upon Tuckman's stages, and combined Norming and Performing into one stage, and added two new stages called Outperforming and Adjourning. A team in the Outperforming stage is also called a high-performing team.

We can apply these group development stages to team formation. As team leaders, we can accelerate our team through the early stages to get to Outperforming faster by implementing these six strategies:

- Encourage relationship building among team members
- Enable team bonding
- Create a shared vision and shared goals
- Facilitate the creation of team norms and agreements
- Form a safe and positive culture
- Foster open-minded communication and discussions

If you already have an established team, it's never too late to *build the team.* Whether you have a new or established team, move your team to high-performing by implementing the strategies explained in this chapter.

ENCOURAGE RELATIONSHIP BUILDING AMONG TEAM MEMBERS

A high-performing team has great rapport and trust, and members work well together to get things done. The best way to create a high-performing team is to foster relationship building between and among team members.

There are many benefits when team members develop strong relationships. The more team members know each other, the more likely they are to trust each other and commit to each other and the team. Team members with a strong sense of camaraderie enjoy working together. Team members are also more likely to adjust their work styles to accommodate their team.

When team members understand each other's aspirations and goals, they will encourage and support each other.

Instead of being competitive, team members with strong relationships are more likely to coordinate on shared goals. They are more likely to combine their abilities and skills to get things done.

Strong relationships also lead to high levels of communication, openness, and understanding. Team members with strong relationships also have more empathy and less judgment. They can read each other's moods and are more open to working together on issues.

When issues emerge, a cohesive team is more likely to give each other the benefit of the doubt. This allows the team to overcome conflict and challenges together.

As the team leader, you can encourage your team members to build strong quality relationships. Give the team time to get to know each other, and support them in doing so. Like you learned in Practice 4, the best way to build relationships and grow them over time is to meet often. Schedule regular team meetings once a week and devote part of the agenda to relationship building so the team can get to know each other as individuals.

In Jon Gordon's book *The Power of Positive Leadership*, he tells the story of a leader who invites a different individual at each team meeting to sit in the "safe seat." The leader asks the individual to share either a defining moment, who his or her hero is, or a hardship they have faced. Once they share, the rest of the team can ask questions. It's important that the team understand that what members share does not leave the room. The team also needs to understand sharing can be a vulnerable thing to do, and the team needs to hold the intention of safety, empathy, and non-judgment.

In their book *Building the Team Organization*, Tjosvold and Tjosvold recommend team members sit in a circle with no table between them during team meetings. This "knee-to-knee, eye-to-eye" approach makes getting to know each other easier and communication easier because people can see each other's non-verbal messages.

Also, encourage team members to get to know each other one-on-one, either through team building exercises where you pair people up or at networking events such as a team lunch or an ice cream social.

You may think all this team building and relationship building will take a lot of time. Yes, relationship building takes time. Yet, it's important to invest the time to unite and connect your team in order to build a high-performing team. The high level of productivity and collective decision-making and problem-solving of a high-performing team will make the investment worth it.

I love the saying "go slow to go fast." When you make time to develop and nurture strong relationships, your team will make up for that time with increased coordination and productivity. The team will also spend less time dealing with conflicts and disagreements.

ENABLE TEAM BONDING

Like sports teams, you can enable team bonding by having your team come up with a team name. You may be rolling your eyes or imagining your team members will when you ask them to do this.

Each team has its own unique personality, style, and character. Having a team name can reflect this uniqueness. Creating a team name can also be a fun team building exercise that can generate a few laughs.

Soon after the team is formed, ask them to come up with a team name. Ask individuals to brainstorm team names on their own and then discuss each of them as a team. The discussion may lead to other ideas. Have the team talk about each idea before narrowing down to the one everyone can agree on. Once you have a team name, find a team member willing to create a logo for the team.

Let the team create other ways to bond. For example, they could bond over a shared interest in an element of pop culture. I once had a team that bonded over Marvel Comics characters.

CREATE A SHARED VISION AND SHARED GOALS

It's important for team members to have a shared understanding of the team's objectives and goals. Being part of a team with a shared effort toward a shared goal can be a rewarding experience for employees.

Having a shared team vision is also important. This shared vision starts with you, the team leader. The best way for you to create this shared vision with your team is to leverage the trust you have created with them as shown in Practice 4. That trust can go a long way. Many leadership influencers believe people don't follow the vision, they follow leaders because they trust and like them.

The first step is to align your leadership purpose with your vision for the team and to share this vision with the team. The next step is to ask the team to discuss your vision and come up with a shared team vision, one that each member agrees to. Ask them if they're inspired by the vision. If not, keep sharing ideas until everyone buys into the shared vision. This shared vision can be a North Star for the team, and something they can align and work together on.

Once you have a team vision, it's your responsibility as the team leader to hold this vision for the team. Help the team work together and take action to move toward that vision. Remind the team of the team vision because this may help the team overcome challenges or conflicts that arise.

FACILITATE THE CREATION OF TEAM NORMS AND AGREEMENTS

Like a shared vision, it's important for team leaders to facilitate the creation of common norms and agreements for how the team will work together.

Norms are rules about how a group is expected to work together and behave toward each other. Agreements are like ground rules. The team should talk about and choose norms and agreements.

Here are examples of team norms and agreements:

- Treat others with respect
- Listen first to understand

- Strive to be open-minded and understand each other's perspectives
- Practice empathy and put yourself in others' shoes
- Give each other the benefit of the doubt
- Be accountable to the team
- Have fun and celebrate the wins

When you facilitate the team's process for choosing norms and agreements, be sure to share your own expectations for the team.

Set aside time in the early weeks of the team's formation to talk about norms and agreements. If you wait too long, unwritten norms may form, and these may not be healthy norms.

The process of choosing norms and agreements may take two or more two-hour sessions. The larger the team, the more time you will need.

Here is a six-step process you can use with your team:

1. At an early meeting, begin the discussion on norms and agreements by asking your team the following questions:

   - What kind of team do you want to be?
   - What kind of team culture do you want to have?
   - What does this team stand for?
   - What does this team want to be known for?

- How will you work together as a team to find solutions when problems or conflicts arise?

2. At the end of the first meeting on norms and agreements, give each team member the assignment to think about and list what norms and agreements they would like for the team.

3. Before the second meeting on norms and agreements, compile the team member's lists. Flag the norms and agreements shared by two or more people and combine similar norms and agreements.

4. At the second meeting, have the team discuss the norms and agreements that two or more team members listed. Then, have the team explore other norms and agreements team members think the team should include. Make sure each team member supports the norms and agreements. The team's final list is not complete until all members of the team have discussed them and agreed to them.

5. If at the end of the second meeting, there is still disagreement, schedule another meeting to continue the discussion.

During future team meetings, ask the team to share how the norms and agreements are helping the team. Also, talk about any conflicts and identify the need for additional norms or agreements.

Along with norms and agreements, facilitate the creation of a Team Charter. The purpose of the Team Charter is to document how the team will work together, and includes the vision, norms, and agreements. The team develops the Team Charter together. Examples of components of a Team Charter are:

- Team vision, objectives, and goals
- Norms and agreements
- Team communication plan
- Roles and responsibilities

FORM A SAFE AND POSITIVE CULTURE

The team's norms and agreements can have a positive impact on team culture. Team leaders can also set expectations for a safe and positive culture, and lead by example.

Culture shows up as a display of behaviors and habits. Behind culture are expectations and beliefs. A safe team culture is one where team members feel safe to be open, and it allows people to learn and grow. More innovation and success will result when people have the freedom to share their ideas and opinions. A positive team culture is one that energizes and encourages team members to do their best work and reach their goals.

Make sure you do the work to stay positive and create a safe space around you. It takes energy and focus to create a positive and safe culture. You must sustain your efforts as the team leader and reinforce a safe and positive culture every day. Your attitude and energy can be contagious.

You can also have the expectation that every team member takes responsibility for their role in shaping team culture. Address any negativity or behavior that impacts the team's sense of safety right away. Don't ignore it. Don't let negativity breed and grow in your team.

Implement a no-complaining rule. For example, no one can complain unless they also offer one or more possible solutions.

FOSTER OPEN-MINDED COMMUNICATION AND DISCUSSIONS

A team that understands, values, and practices open-mindedness is a team that will make better decisions, solve problems, and resolve conflicts.

A team can have diverse ideas. Open-minded discussions help team members combine their ideas and learn together so they can find good solutions and make good decisions. The increase in the number of ideas and stimulation from open-minded discussions fosters creativity and innovation.

Open-mindedness also builds trust. When people believe others see them and hear them, they feel important and valued. With open-minded discussions, team members feel good about the process, the decision, and their team members.

Open-minded communication is listening to understand what someone is saying. Team members must be able to express their frustrations and opinions and feel heard and understood. Open-mindedness is asking clarifying questions to understand what is being said. It's also suspending judgment and practicing empathy.

It is inevitable for conflict to occur, but when managed well, conflict can be good for the team. If the team has an unresolved conflict, it can impact collaboration, productivity, and morale. When team members have conflict or disagreements, communication is the best solution.

Team leaders can foster open-minded communication and open-minded discussions in team decision-making and problem-solving.

Allow time during regular team meetings for team members to talk about and resolve conflicts. Help the team identify issues and dig into them.

Have the team discuss conflict open-mindedly to learn and understand the reasons behind the conflict. Help the team consider potential solutions and agree on a solution. Remind the team of its shared vision and goals and encourage compromise and resolution. When the team resolves a conflict with a positive outcome, celebrate the win.

Your team can have effective open-minded discussions when each team member agrees to:

- Focus on the team's common goals and shared vision
- View every team member as having an equal role in decision-making
- Contribute to team discussions and share concerns
- Listen more than they speak
- See issues from multiple perspectives
- Work with their team members to define the problem and find solutions
- Seek to understand with empathy, and search for a new understanding and information by asking questions
- Show respect and acceptance of others, even when there is disagreement
- Synthesize different ideas to form a new position not yet considered

FURTHER LEARNING

Building the Team Organization: How to Open Minds, Resolve Conflict, and Ensure Cooperation by Dean Tjosvold and Mary Tjosvold

The Power of Positive Leadership: How and Why Positive Leaders Transform Teams and Organizations and Change the World by Jon Gordon

KEY TAKEAWAYS

- Facilitate the creation of a shared vision, one that inspires every team member and can become the team's North Star.
- Encourage team members to get to know each other well and develop strong quality relationships, which will increase cooperation and coordination.
- Foster a safe and positive culture, facilitate the creation of team norms and agreements, and encourage open-minded discussions.

COMING UP IN PRACTICE 6: DELEGATE EFFECTIVELY WITH CLEAR EXPECTATIONS AND CANDID FEEDBACK

Effective delegation begins with setting goals and expectations and continues with ongoing support and feedback. Practice 6 walks through the practice of delegating, providing feedback well, and what to do when performance is subpar. Also, not to miss is the section on how to avoid making fundamental attribution errors and self-fulfilling prophecies.

DELEGATE EFFECTIVELY WITH CLEAR EXPECTATIONS AND FEEDBACK

"People who feel good about themselves produce good results."
– Ken Blanchard and Spencer Johnson,
The New One Minute Manager

HIGH EXPECTATIONS AND HIGH SUPPORT

Early in my role as a team leader, I stumbled upon *The One Minute Manager* by Ken Blanchard and Spencer Johnson. This book was re-published in 2015 with the name *The New One Minute Manager*. I believe reading that book was the foundation for my success as a team leader. Through a compelling story, the book shows that combining high expectations with a high level of support is the best way to lead people.

I also learned from *The New One Minute Manager* that most performance issues occur when the team leader does not give clear expectations or adequate training. It's rare that bad performance is due to a lack of competence or a bad attitude.

In this chapter, you'll learn how to delegate and give feedback while providing team members with a high level of support. You'll also learn what to do when someone is not meeting expectations, and how to avoid making fundamental attribution errors and self-fulfilling prophecies.

DELEGATION BEGINS WITH SETTING GOALS AND CLEAR EXPECTATIONS

When we delegate, it's important to give clear expectations. For each assignment, we need to make sure we communicate the expected:

- Goals
- Level of quality
- Deadline
- Priority level compared to the person's other assignments
- Level of autonomy in performing the work
- Milestones and review points
- Frequency of progress updates

The amount of time we spend with someone to set goals and clarify expectations for an assignment depends on the person's experience and expertise. If we assign something to a new team member who lacks experience, we need to document the process and give detailed instructions. For a team member who has done similar work before, we won't need to give instructions. Instead, we can let the person set their own goals for the assignment.

When delegating, we want to make sure the team member takes ownership of the assignment. We also want her to see the value to her and to the team of doing the assignment and doing it well. Thus, it's best to delegate whole projects or big chunks of projects, instead of individual tasks. Even though the person owns the assignment, they can still coordinate with other team members on getting the work done.

SITUATIONAL SUPPORT

We need to be flexible in our approach to delegation depending on the situation.

Once we've set clear expectations and goals for the assignment, the level of support we give will depend on the person's level of experience and their past performance. Our level of support may also depend on whether the person has done this type of work before or if they will need to learn a new skill.

We need to decide if the person needs any on-the-job training or other resources to complete the assignment. We should ask the person to tell us if they run into obstacles or if they have questions.

As the team leader, our job is to help clear the path of obstacles. To clear the path, we can help solve a problem or find additional training or resources.

We also need to share our communication preferences with our team. For things that come up between scheduled check-in meetings, we need to state whether we prefer team members drop by our desk, call us, or email us. Advise the team if there are certain times or situations where we don't want them to get in touch with us. These times may include after work hours or during our blocks of focused work time.

HOLD TEAM MEMBERS ACCOUNTABLE

When we hold team members accountable for quality and timeline expectations, this helps move the team forward and creates more engagement. The best way to hold team members accountable is to hold weekly team meetings. People tend to be accountable to others, but not to themselves. When their team members count on them to get their work done, they are more likely to work hard to meet their commitments.

During team meetings, each team member reports on their progress in meeting their commitments from the prior week. They share what went well and where they struggled, and they share and celebrate their accomplishments. Each team member also shares their commitments for the week ahead.

When someone does not meet their commitments, they're given the opportunity to share why they didn't meet them and what challenges they faced. With respect and empathy, the team and the team leader listens to the person. The team leader clarifies expectations and tells the person the team counts on everyone to meet their commitments and asks the person to recommit to a new deadline.

Team meetings are also a good time for the team to check in on progress toward its bigger goals. The team checks in with their overall vision and objectives, and talks about how things are going.

It's important for team leaders to share progress on their own commitments and to meet their own deadlines. This creates trust with the team and shows that the team leader can demonstrate accountability while also holding others accountable.

Team leaders can also use weekly team meetings to clarify quality and deadline expectations, help identify resource needs, and anticipate problems.

Team meetings can also give team members the opportunity to coordinate and help each other. For example, Sarah may be skilled in a software program that Eric needs to learn to complete an assignment. The two of them can coordinate on a time so Sarah can train Eric on how to use the software.

BEWARE OF MICROMANAGEMENT AND ABSENTEE MANAGEMENT

In Practice 3, you learned about the pitfalls of micromanagement from Chris's story. Chris was her team's best and most productive worker and was promoted to team leader. Yet, Chris learned she wasn't prepared to be a successful team leader, and took more of a directive and micromanagement approach. Her team went from the best performing team in the organization to the worst. Her team members' morale dropped, and they felt unsupported and untrusted.

Micromanagement is being hands-on and focused on the details. When someone micromanages, she solves other people's problems and speaks more than listens.

Just as bad is to swing too far in the opposite direction. Absentee management is being too hands-off. It is when someone is clueless about what his team members are working on and the status of their assignments. He is also not aware of problems or issues. Team members are also unclear about expectations and whether they're meeting those expectations.

LINK FEEDBACK TO EXPECTATIONS AND GOALS

Once we've set clear goals and expectations for our team members, we need to give them ongoing feedback. Feedback reinforces expectations, and we should always link feedback to an expectation or professional development goal.

We may realize we did not set a specific expectation related to the feedback we're about to give. When this occurs, we will need to share the expectation.

In my experience, team members want more feedback than they are given. The purpose of feedback is so team members learn when they're meeting expectations and when they're not. It's important to give both positive praise and constructive feedback.

Our feedback should be encouraging. We should base our feedback on both high expectations and a high level of confidence in the person's abilities. Team members will be more confident and feel valued when we give feedback in a way that encourages and supports them. We can help our team members grow and develop when we deliver feedback well.

MODEL RECEIVING FEEDBACK WELL

As team leaders, we need to understand that receiving critical feedback can be difficult. We can model receiving feedback well by asking our team for feedback and showing we are open to the feedback with our behavior and response. We don't want to be defensive or minimize the feedback.

If we show we can receive feedback well, we can be that model for our team, and we can also build trust with our team. If we show we don't receive feedback well, we cannot expect our team members to receive it well either. We will also erode trust, and our team members will be less comfortable giving us feedback.

GIVE PRAISE TO REINFORCE EXPECTATIONS

The frequency and type of feedback we give to our team members depends on their level of experience. This is similar to how we adjust our level of direction and support when setting goals and delegating assignments.

For a new hire or when a team member is learning a new skill, we want to begin by focusing on giving positive feedback. We want to give praise when the person meets expectations or makes progress toward meeting expectations. Praise reinforces these expectations and encourages good future performance.

We also want to give praise as soon as possible after we see good work or when someone is doing something well. When we see someone doing something right, we tell them. Otherwise, the person may not realize they've met expectations and may try something different next time, which may take them off track.

In all cases, we want to give much more praise than constructive feedback. There is no exact formula, but we want to avoid sandwiching constructive feedback between two layers of praise. The goal is to give sincere praise. When we sandwich feedback, people may feel manipulated. If we have both praise and constructive feedback to give, then we should give praise first and point out everything they are doing well.

REDIRECT WITH CRITICISM AND CONSTRUCTIVE FEEDBACK

Constructive feedback is when we point out where the person needs to improve to meet an expectation or goal.

As with positive feedback, it's important constructive feedback is timely. We don't want to save up all our feedback to deliver at one time. For example, we don't want to save up constructive feedback for someone's six-month or annual performance evaluation.

With constructive feedback, we should deliver it in a private and non-threatening space. We also want to give a context for the feedback. Like praise, we should link constructive feedback to an expectation or goal. We also want to show our support in the person and share our confidence in the person. For example, consider this conversation from a team leader to one of her team members:

"Sue, we talked about your goal of becoming a more effective speaker, and your focus on making more eye contact when you're speaking. I know this is important to you. I'd like to share feedback on your performance in the management team meeting today. During your presentation, I saw you look around the room and look each person in the eye. You smiled a lot, and you hit all the important points of your presentation. Your speaking has improved a great deal. I'm proud of you. At the end of your presentation, when you answered questions, I noticed you looked at the ground a lot and looked through your notes to find the answers. I have confidence in you and you're very knowledgeable about this project. What was going on? What do you think you could do next time to be more confident when answering management questions? Let me know how I can help."

In the above scenario, the team leader gave the context for the feedback by talking about the goal. The team leader also shared where the person had made improvements in her public speaking. When the team leader delivered the constructive feedback, she told Sue she had confidence in her. She also didn't give all the answers; instead, she asked Sue questions about how she thinks she could improve. Then the team leader ended by asking how she could help.

HOW TO GIVE FEEDBACK WELL

Like recognizing when to give feedback, it's important to understand how to give feedback well.

Feedback is a two-step process: preparation and delivery.

1. Preparation

- Identify the performance or behavior you're addressing. Focus on facts, behaviors, or actions, but not on the person.
- Identify the expectation and assess whether you delivered the expectation.
- Note specific examples from your observations. Where did the work product or behavior not meet expectations, and where did it hit the mark?
- Whether the person met expectations or not, explore the impact of the performance or behavior on you or the team.
- Identify ways you can express and give support and encouragement.

2. Delivery

- Explain the performance or behavior you're addressing, and which goal or expectation it relates to.

- Acknowledge if you did not give the expectation and take the time to share the expectation.
- Be as specific as you can when you give feedback. Tell the person what they did right and encourage the person to continue performing at that level. For constructive feedback, tell the person where they did not meet expectations.
- Describe specific examples from your observations of how the behavior or performance did or did not meet expectations.
- Ask the other person their perspective. Ask them what they think and confirm your facts and observations are correct.
- Explain the impact of the behavior or performance on you or the team. If you're giving praise, tell them their behavior or work product is what you expect and should become the standard.
- Express support and encouragement. The focus of feedback should be on building confidence and competence. With constructive feedback, tell them you know they can do better. Ask them how you can better support them. Coach them in how they can make improvements. With positive feedback, tell them you knew they could do it.

FEEDBACK METHODS TO AVOID

It goes without saying, but we never want to use feedback as a put-down. We need to focus on the behavior, not the person.

We also want to avoid the "Leave-Alone-Zap" technique as described by Blanchard and Johnson. This technique occurs when we don't give regular feedback and instead give negative feedback only when we see someone doing something wrong. It is not an effective way to motivate staff when we only give corrective feedback and don't give praise when warranted.

CREATE A FEEDBACK CULTURE

Now that you understand how to receive and deliver feedback well, share and train your team members in these methods. Show how to give and receive feedback. One way to do this is to hold a team building session where the team practices giving and receiving feedback based on example scenarios. Have team members take turns being the feedback giver and feedback receiver.

Once your team has practiced giving and receiving feedback, encourage a feedback culture. Encourage feedback in all directions and on an ongoing basis. Ask your team to share feedback with you, and to trade off asking for and receiving feedback from others.

ADDRESS POOR PERFORMANCE

When performance is subpar, it's likely because of an unclear expectation, inexperience, or a skill gap. It's rare for attitude or inability to be the main cause of poor performance.

If we set clear goals and expectations and give a high level of support, we can help prevent poor performance.

We may still find ourselves with a team member who produces poor quality work or does not meet other expectations. When this happens, we may need to become more directive and supportive, and spend more time with them. We need to get in front of the performance issue. We don't want to let even one deadline or issue with quality slip.

For ongoing issues with poor performance, you need to work with the person to develop a performance improvement plan. This includes identifying the skill gap or behavior that needs improvement. While creating the plan, you also want to talk about expectations and consequences.

After you create a performance improvement plan with your team member, schedule regular one-on-one meetings to check progress. Give ongoing feedback during and outside of scheduled meetings. Constant feedback is key. Give praise when they meet the expectation and when you see their behavior improve. At first, you may need to praise them even if they're only halfway there. Also, give feedback in the areas they are still not meeting expectations and coach them to correct the behavior or the work.

Most important is to express your confidence in the person, and to show you respect and support them. When we see someone's potential and express that potential, they are more likely to see it too.

BEWARE OF FUNDAMENTAL ATTRIBUTION ERRORS AND SELF-FULFILLING PROPHECIES

A fundamental attribution error is when we believe someone's behaviors reflect who they are; for example, when we label someone as a flake because they are late for meetings. Instead of focusing on the specific behaviors, we focus on a person's personality or character traits.

To prevent us from falling into the fundamental attribution error trap, we need to remember to focus on behaviors and avoid labeling people. When we label someone, this creates a belief that the person cannot change. Instead, we should focus on the behavior and give candid feedback. This gives them the opportunity to correct the behavior.

Another trap is the self-fulfilling prophecy. A self-fulfilling prophecy is when we make a prediction based on our beliefs. Then we alter our behavior based on that prediction, which causes the prediction to come true. Our prediction causes us to act in ways that directly or indirectly bring about the consequences we expect.

For example, if we believe someone has great potential and predict they do well, we are more likely to give them more of our support. We may take them under our wing and give them opportunities to grow and develop. Our actions are thus more likely to lead them to meet our expectations.

Yet, if a new team member makes a mistake early on, we may believe they are not competent enough and predict they will be a poor performer. This belief may cause us to distrust and micromanage the person. We are less likely to give them growth and development opportunities. Our behavior and actions are likely to impact the person's self-confidence and they may be less willing to take initiative or to take risks. Their behavior becomes a reaction to our behavior. Thus, they will show up as we expect them to, and our prediction will come true.

Early in my career, I had a boss who seemed to have low expectations of me. This was after I held a prior job where my boss gave me a lot of autonomy and showed trust and confidence in me. Yet, my new boss acted as if he had little trust or confidence in me. On one occasion, I made what I thought was a minor mistake, but my boss criticized me. I felt incompetent, and I became averse to taking risks or making my own decisions. I asked a lot of questions because I didn't want to make another mistake. In hindsight, I realized my boss had decided what he could expect from me and acted on that expectation.

It's important to be mindful of first impressions and to treat each person as if they have the potential to be a high performer. Have high expectations for all your team members and give them the same level of support and guidance. Each person may not have the same competency, but everyone has potential. It may surprise you how well your team members rise to meet your expectations for high-performance.

FURTHER LEARNING

The New One Minute Manager by Ken Blanchard and Spencer Johnson

Radical Candor: Be a Kick-Ass Boss Without Losing Your Humanity by Kim Scott

Thanks for the Feedback: The Science and Art of Receiving Feedback Well by Douglas Heen and Sheila Stone

KEY TAKEAWAYS

- Delegate to your team well by setting high expectations and giving a high level of support.
- Give ongoing and supportive feedback so team members see where they are meeting expectations and where they can improve and develop.

- Beware of fundamental attribution errors and self-fulfilling prophecies and understand that most poor performance is because of unclear expectations or lack of skill.

COMING UP IN PRACTICE 7: COACH YOUR TEAM TO EXTRAORDINARY RESULTS

What would it be like to have a team with high rapport and high productivity that produces amazing results? Team leaders can achieve high-performance by coaching their team. In the next chapter, you will learn the payoffs and components of effective coaching. You will also learn how to coach your team to manage itself. A self-managing team decides how they can best work together, help each other out, make decisions, and solve problems.

COACH YOUR TEAM TO HIGH-PERFORMANCE

"Coaching is unlocking people's potential to maximize their own performance. It is helping them to learn rather than teaching them."
– John Whitmore, *Coaching for Performance*

REACHING HIGH-PERFORMANCE

The day I realized my team had become a high-performing team, I was in awe. I was thrilled. The level of open communication was high. Everyone was taking responsibility. Rapport and morale were also high. We were not just team members, we were comrades. We worked well together, produced work at a fast pace, and achieved exceptional results.

My team members and I were state performance auditors, and we were auditing community college completion rates.

The pinnacle moment for the team occurred after a difficult meeting with our management team. The purpose of the meeting was to discuss the scope and direction of the audit. We had proposed our scope ideas to management, but our management team pushed back on our ideas. The meeting ended with no agreement.

After the meeting, my team and I huddled in a conference room to talk about what went wrong. We were in it together. We realized we didn't prepare well enough for the meeting and were not persuasive. Each one of us took responsibility for our part. We each shared what we could have done differently. We learned a lot from this, and the team pulled closer together.

Two weeks later, we met with management again. We were better prepared and management approved our project scope.

BE YOUR TEAM'S COACH

You are the team's leader and you are also the team's coach. It's your responsibility to develop and coach each team member.

Coaching allows team members to develop new skills and increase confidence so they can be full contributors to the team. Coaching also creates the foundation for high-performing teams. A coached team will be more engaged and work together to produce exceptional results.

Invest in coaching your team members and they will feel valued and more connected with the team. They will also have more motivation and job satisfaction.

Coaching involves trusting your team members and understanding they are all capable and have great potential. They have everything they need, you just need to help pull it out of them. If you have confidence in them, they will have confidence in themselves.

You will also benefit from coaching your team members. It's rewarding to help others grow and learn. You can have a direct impact on your team member's careers and lives. I remember the first time one of my team members was promoted to team leader after I coached and mentored her. It was rewarding to watch her confidence and skills grow. I watched her transition well into the role of team leader.

WHAT IS COACHING?

First, what coaching is not. It is not giving the answers or solutions.

It's easy to give your team the answers. Yet, coaching takes conscious listening and asking questions.

When coaching, you are helping the person become more effective in their current role and preparing them for success in future roles. Coaching inspires people to reach their full potential and guides them past obstacles so they can reach their career goals.

Coaching is putting the responsibility for personal development, problem-solving, and decision-making on individual team members. As a coach, you guide them to grow their abilities and give them the confidence to solve problems on their own. In time, you can also coach them to coach themselves.

COMPONENTS OF EFFECTIVE COACHING

1. Create a coaching relationship

Coaching is most effective when you've established and built a solid relationship with the person you're coaching. It's important to invest time in the relationship.

You want to build trust with the person and make sure the person feels safe enough to be open and honest with you. Get to know the whole person during your one-on-ones and show you care by being interested and asking questions about their personal lives. Show you are invested in the person's success and use the person's goals and dreams as the context for coaching.

2. Understand team members' dreams

In Practice 4, you learned how important it is to learn your team member's life stories. As you do that, listen for what they value and how their values motivate them.

As you build trust with your team members and show you want to support their growth and development, ask them to share their dreams. Ask them:

- What does success mean to you?
- What will success look like for you in your current position?
- Where do you want to be at the peak of your career?

3. Assess strengths and weaknesses and set short- and long-term goals

To help your team member succeed in their current position, share your expectations and how you will evaluate her performance. Work with your team member to identify and set goals related to her current position.

Assess each person's strengths, weaknesses, and potential. Work with them to identify their strengths and what they want to build on. Identify improvements needed in specific skill or behavioral areas that will help them grow and do well in their current role.

The next step is to identify additional skills, knowledge, and experience needed for them to reach their dreams. Help them set long-term goals.

Help the person to identify a five-year goal that, if achieved, will get them closer to their dream. Then help them identify a one-year goal that, if achieved, will help them achieve their five-year goal. Next, identify the skills, knowledge, and experience they will need to reach their one-year goal.

Together, make a one-year plan for training, on-the-job experience, and stretch assignments. Identify training needs, tools, or other resources they might need. Be their champion and request training resources for them.

If appropriate, pair your team member up with a mentor whose experience and position align with their dream. Tailor your team member's assignments to get her the experience she needs to move closer to achieving her goals. Encourage your team member to be proactive and seek training and other experiences on her own.

Link the person's short- and long-term goals to the team's goals. Explore how the team's achievements will link back to the team member's personal achievements.

4. Make coaching your priority and be prepared

Free up time in your schedule for coaching. Make time for both one-on-one coaching meetings and informal coaching throughout the day. If you make time for coaching your team, this investment will lead to increased productivity and results.

Before coaching meetings or informal coaching conversations, take the time to center yourself and prepare. Manage your own emotions and be present.

Prepare by going over the person's goals and the last conversation you had with them.

Make sure you're in a positive frame of mind. The person you're coaching needs to believe you are focused and interested in them and their success. Making a positive emotional connection with the person requires you to be present and engaged in the conversation.

Make sure there are also no distractions and you won't be interrupted during your conversation.

5. Listen and ask questions

Coaching is mostly listening. Let the person lead the conversation. Ask open-ended questions. Ask clarifying questions and paraphrase back to confirm your understanding.

Give your full attention and give the person the time to think and respond. Be patient and avoid jumping in to share your own thoughts.

Coaching conversations can include helping someone solve a problem, decide how best to complete an assignment, develop a skill, or work toward a goal.

For problem-solving, ask questions to help them see what's behind the problem or the cause of the problem. Have the person think and come up with and consider different solutions even if it means there are pauses where neither of you talks. This helps the person improve their problem-solving and analytical skills.

When people find their own solutions, they are more likely to follow through and own the result. Imagine if you gave advice that someone implemented, and it backfired. You would then own the result because it was your idea.

As the person identifies solutions or considers different decisions, ask them to weigh each thing they come up with.

Support their solutions and check back in with them on how it went. Did their solution work? What did they learn?

If a team member makes a mistake, coach them by asking what went wrong, how they can avoid making the mistake again, and what they would do differently next time.

If it's appropriate to give constructive feedback, be sure to follow the methods described in Practice 6. Make sure your feedback is clear and without judgment.

COACH YOUR TEAM TO SELF-MANAGEMENT

The path to a high-performing team that produces exceptional results is to help your team become a self-managing team. A self-managing team decides how they can best work together, make decisions, and solve problems.

Teams that have moved through the basic formation stages and are performing well may be ready to self-manage. Teams that self-manage require the team leader to give them the autonomy to make their own decisions about how they will meet goals and get the work done.

Helping a team become self-managing has many benefits. When the team makes its own decisions, it has more ownership over each decision and a sense of responsibility to the team and its success. Another benefit to becoming self-managing is an increase in the team's growth and development.

When teams problem-solve and make decisions together, they become more connected and unified. In turn, more connection and unity will enable the team to work better together.

You can prepare your team for self-management by coaching them to coach themselves. This includes teaching them how to ask themselves questions. If they still need guidance, tell them your door is always open.

Moving your team toward self-management requires that you share leadership, create a flat team, and push decision-making down to the team as much as possible. The number and level of decisions you push down to your team will grow as you and your team gain confidence in the team's abilities.

In Practice 7, we explored team decision-making through open-minded discussions. As your team practices open-minded discussions and making decisions together, coach them to facilitate themselves. When teams can talk about issues open-mindedly to get things done, make decisions, and solve conflicts, they will be self-managing.

FURTHER LEARNING

Coaching for Performance: GROWing Human Potential and Purpose – the Principles and Practice of Coaching and Leadership by John Whitmore
The Coaching Habit: Say Less, Ask More & Change the Way You Lead Forever by Michael Bungay Stanier

KEY TAKEAWAYS

- Coaching is both helping people become more effective in their current roles and helping prepare them for success in future roles.
- The path to a high-performing team is to coach your team to become a self-managing team.
- A self-managing team decides how they can best work together, make decisions, and problem solve.

COMING UP IN PART III: LEAD YOUR BOSS

Like leading ourselves and leading our team, our success depends on how well we lead our boss. In Part III, you will learn how to create a strong relationship with your boss and how to get clear on your boss's expectations for you and your team.

PART 3
LEAD YOUR BOSS

BUILD A STRONG RELATIONSHIP WITH YOUR BOSS

"Establishing strong, productive working relationships is the single most effective way to accelerate success in any organization."
– Mary Abbajay, *Managing Up*

TWO DIFFERENT SCENARIOS, TWO DIFFERENT RELATIONSHIPS

What if you could have a relationship with your boss that allowed you to be candid with them, and them with you? A relationship where you could be yourself, make mistakes, and be open and honest about those mistakes and where you can improve.

Imagine two different scenarios where at the end of a management team meeting, your boss pulls you aside and says, "You sounded like a fool in there."

One manager asked you a question during the meeting about your project's objective that you were not prepared for. At that moment, you realized you never got clarity on the objective with your boss. You stuttered out, "Uh, uh, I'm not sure. Um, that's a good question," and then deferred to your boss.

In the first scenario, you don't know your boss well and are nervous when you speak to her. You've been in your position for only six months. You don't meet with her often. When you meet with her, you mostly talk about your assignments. It seems like the only time your boss stops by your desk is to suggest improvements to your work. It shocked and hurt you when your boss said, "You sounded like a fool in there." Tears welled up as you said, "Can we talk about this later?" The last thing you want is to cry in front of your boss.

In the second scenario, you have a great relationship with your boss. You've been in your position for a couple years. Once a month, you meet your boss for coffee to share personal stories, talk about each of your professional goals, and trade feedback. Every day, you make sure you greet your boss and chat for a few minutes, either about your project or life outside of work. After your boss said, "You sounded like a fool in there," you laughed.

"Yup, I totally screwed up in there," you said. "Do you have a few minutes to debrief with me this afternoon? I'd like your help and feedback to see what went wrong and what I can do differently next time."

She said, "Of course. How about 3:30 in my office?"

You went back to your desk feeling both frustrated over your performance in the meeting and supported by your boss.

Both these scenarios had the same response from each boss but had two different circumstances and outcomes.

I'm not sure a boss should ever say, "You sounded like a fool in there." If they do, let's hope it's within the context of good intentions and a strong relationship.

You're not always going to have a boss who will focus on relationship building, so it's up to you to be proactive and work to create a strong relationship with your boss.

GET TO KNOW YOUR BOSS AND BUILD THE RELATIONSHIP

Our success and our team's success depends on the quality of our relationship with the person we report to. As with our team members, having a strong relationship with our boss will make open and honest communication, conflict resolution, and receiving feedback much easier.

In his book *Decoding the Workplace,* Dr. John Ballard said, "An effective relationship with your boss increases the likelihood of success in your job."

The method for building a relationship with our boss is like building a relationship with each member of our team as described in Practice 4.

We don't want to depend on our boss to take the lead to develop and nurture a relationship with us. We need to be proactive.

Talk with your boss. Explain to your boss what you'd like to do. Explain your desire to get to know him better, and how important it is for you to have a strong relationship with him. Tell your boss you also want to create a strong partnership with him.

Request he agrees to meet with you at least once a month, and schedule one-on-one meetings with him. If your boss has room in his schedule, weekly is better, even if you only meet for 30 minutes. When feasible, get away from the office. A great option is to meet at a coffee shop.

The fastest way to get to know each other is to share your life stories. Ask your boss to share his life story with you, and the journey he took to get to where he is now. Ask him what experiences have most shaped him, and who his biggest influencers were. As with your team members, actively listen, and ask follow-up questions.

Once your boss has shared, ask if you can share a few stories of your own. Your boss is more apt to connect with you and like you if they know you and what's important to you. Share your stories from your heart. Be open and share the difficult times you've had, and how you overcame challenges to become who you are today.

If this kind of sharing sounds scary and vulnerable to you, understand this is the point. Being vulnerable is necessary to create the personal human connections you want to make with your boss and your team members. If you're afraid of being this vulnerable, you can begin with less vulnerable stories. As you get to know your boss and trust them, maybe you'll be more open with them.

SHARE STRENGTHS AND ASPIRATIONS

Besides getting to know who your boss is and how she got to be where she is, you also want to learn your boss's strengths, aspirations, and goals. Once you learn your boss's personal goals, you can become one of her supporters and find ways to help her.

Also, share your strengths and aspirations with your boss. Share your skills and talents. Share what you're great at, and how you can help the team and the organization.

As with your team members, share what you have learned about yourself from the work you did in Practice 1. Share your limiting belief, blind spots, and strengths. Also, share the areas you're working to improve.

Share the leadership purpose you developed in Practice 2 and ask your boss if she has a leadership purpose or a vision for the team.

ONGOING INVESTMENT IN THE RELATIONSHIP

Like your team members, once you build the relationship with your boss, you'll want to maintain it. Go out of your way every day to connect with your boss. For example, drop by his desk to ask how he's doing, or send an email to update him on your team's progress.

Your boss is human too, so get to know his personal side. Show genuine interest and ask how his weekend went. Also, ask questions about his life outside of work.

As you and your boss become more connected, loosen up and be yourself around him. Share your personality so he can get to know your true self.

Your time and effort to build and maintain a quality relationship with your boss will not only make your job easier, it will also make your job more enjoyable.

FURTHER LEARNING

Managing Up: How to Move up, Win at Work, and Succeed with Any Type of Boss by Mary Abbajay
Decoding the Workplace: 50 Keys to Understanding People in Organizations by John Ballard, Ph.D.

KEY TAKEAWAYS

- Your success as a team leader and enjoyment at work will depend on the quality of your relationship with the person you report to.
- Be proactive and build a strong relationship with your boss.
- Having a strong relationship with your boss will make communication, resolving conflicts, and asking for and receiving feedback easier.

COMING UP IN PRACTICE 9: LEAD UP

Sometimes we need to lead up. Leading your boss is not about brown-nosing. It's about making sure you're clear on the priorities and expectations your boss has of you and your team. Practice 9 gives you strategies for ensuring you meet expectations, understand priorities, and create a strong alliance with your manager.

PRACTICE 9

LEAD UP

"Leadership has always required more than a downward touch: It needs to come from below as well as from the top, and leaders today must reach up as never before."
– Michael Useem, *Leading Up*

WHAT IS LEADING UP?

As a team leader, leading up wasn't on my radar. I didn't know leading up was a thing or something I needed to practice.

After leading teams during much of my career, I was promoted to a program manager position. In this new position, I learned about leading up and what to do and what not to do.

Here are basic practices of leading up:

- Get clear on expectations
- Understand priorities
- Learn your boss's work styles and communication preferences
- Communicate often
- Request feedback
- Create a strong partnership with your boss

After I learned about these leading up practices, I realized I had already been doing a few of them. As a team leader, I made sure I was clear about my manager's expectations, and I kept my manager informed of my team's progress and accomplishments. I also adapted to the work style of my manager.

Looking back though, I realized I did not regularly ask for constructive feedback.

In one situation, I also failed to create a partnership with my manager and to maintain a strong relationship with him. I'll share more on this story later in the chapter.

Leading our boss is just as important as leading our team. Leading our boss is about creating a strong professional relationship and making sure we are clear on our boss's priorities and expectations.

GET CLEAR ON EXPECTATIONS

To make sure you meet expectations, you need to get clear on your boss's expectations and priorities. Be proactive and talk about expectations at your regular one-on-one meetings with him. Don't assume what your boss's expectations are for you and your team.

Talk to your boss and confirm his expectations related to your team's priorities, objectives, and deadlines. Learn what metrics or performance measures he expects your team to meet. To manage scope creep, get in agreement on the scope of work and meet often with your boss to clarify the scope.

Ask your boss what he will evaluate you on during your annual performance evaluation. If your boss has not yet given you a performance evaluation, ask if you can see the evaluation template.

Get clear on what your boss sees as your roles and responsibilities. Confirm with your boss how much independence you have in conducting your work. Ask what decisions you and your team can make on your own. Find out how much input and involvement your boss wishes to have, and how often your boss wishes to receive progress updates from you.

You're on your boss's team. Be a great team member. Remember those basic expectations you have for your team members and meet those in addition to your boss's expectations.

UNDERSTAND PRIORITIES

Understand your boss's priorities. Seek to understand the unique challenges and pressures she faces. Learn what's most important to your boss. Ask your boss what matters to her, and what success looks like for her. Once you learn your boss's priorities and goals, align your priorities and goals with hers.

Priorities can change. Stay informed about organization-wide changes and shifts in priorities. Be flexible and change your priorities when your boss's priorities change. Sometimes unexpected things arise. Ask your boss to tell you when priorities change or if there's an urgent matter you can help with.

Never assume what your boss's priorities are. Get clarity on her priorities and goals, and how you and your team can help achieve those goals.

LEARN YOUR BOSS'S WORKSTYLES AND COMMUNICATION PREFERENCES

Learn the work styles and communication preferences of your boss and conform to them. Either ask your boss or observe his patterns. When you know your boss's work styles and preferences, you'll be able to work with him better.

Learn his pet peeves and avoid them. If your boss knows his Myers-Briggs temperaments, ask him to share them and how these relate to his work styles and work preferences. Also, ask your boss what his leadership style is.

Sit down with your boss and learn how he prefers to communicate. You should have already established regular one-on-one meetings with your boss. Learn his expectations for how often he wants progress updates. Ask your boss how he prefers to hear from you on a day-to-day basis. For example, does he prefer email, drop-ins, or phone calls when you have urgent questions or problems? Tailor your method of communication to what works best for your boss.

COMMUNICATE OFTEN

Create a communication plan with your boss. Include your regular one-on-one meetings and your regular status updates in your communication plan.

At your one-on-one meetings, use the time to make sure you're meeting your boss's expectations.

Be a connector between your team and your boss. During your regular status updates, include team progress, accomplishments, and what the team will work on next. As needed, clarify expectations and talk about challenges.

Never let your boss be surprised about what you're working on, your progress, or problems. You've learned your boss's communication preferences, and how often she wants status updates from you. Keep your boss up-to-date and give her regular status and progress updates on your assignments and projects. If something comes up in between regular status updates, inform your boss right away.

When you share bad news, share the whole story. Leave nothing out. You want to be transparent to maintain trust and make sure your boss has all the information. Also, don't sugarcoat it.

When you can, talk face-to-face with your boss. Face-to-face allows for full communication and the ability to read your boss's non-verbal cues. You can listen better when you can read nonverbal cues. You can also check in with your boss and check your assumptions if her non-verbal communication did not fit with what she said.

REQUEST FEEDBACK

During your one-on-one meetings, ask your boss for feedback on where you need to improve or where you're not meeting expectations. Have a mindset of continuous growth and improvement. Share your openness to feedback and how it will help you grow and improve.

When your boss gives you feedback, be sure to receive it well. Don't defend yourself. Listen actively and ask follow-up questions to clarify what he said. Repeat back your understanding of the feedback. Be sure to thank your boss after he gives you feedback, and share how you will process the feedback and work to improve. Receiving feedback well helps build trust with your boss, and he is also more likely to continue giving you constructive feedback.

CREATE A STRONG PARTNERSHIP WITH YOUR BOSS

Leading up also includes creating a strong partnership with your boss. This includes helping your boss meet her goals and priorities and being her steadfast supporter.

Show your boss your appreciation and compliment her. Have confidence in her and expect her best, just as you would with your other team members. Recognize her when she is doing a great job or did something you respect.

Be a strong partner by doing your job well. Align your strategies and plans with your boss's goals and priorities. Do what you say you're going to do. Lead your team so they can get the work done and achieve the results expected. If you realize you're not able to meet a deadline or get something done, share this with your boss right away and talk about options. Work to find a solution.

Have a positive "can do" attitude at all times and tell your boss "I've got this handled." Make your boss's job easier by anticipating needs and volunteering to help.

Keep your boss informed and be open and honest. Don't filter or hide information from her. Also, give your boss objective advice.

In partnering with and supporting your boss, ask if she wants to receive feedback from you. If not, don't push it. If she does, follow the steps outlined in Practice 6 for providing effective feedback.

Cooperate and collaborate with your boss. Be open, share your views and concerns, and challenge your boss with respect when appropriate.

When you have different opinions on something, ask your boss if you can each share your different views and seek agreement. Avoid disagreeing with your boss in public. Tell your boss you are sharing your views and concerns because of your commitment to what your boss is trying to achieve. Listen to your boss's point of view and ask questions to understand her views better. If your boss makes a decision you disagree with, after you and your boss exchange views, support her in that decision anyway.

If you have a conflict with your boss or if she does or says something that concerns or impacts you, talk to her about it in person. Try to find resolution with her. Give her the benefit of the doubt and check any assumptions you may have. Put yourself in your boss's shoes and practice empathy.

Work with your boss to resolve conflict. Don't go behind her back and badmouth your boss to others and don't go above her. Only go above your boss after you have done your best to resolve it yourself, and then only if you think what she did or said was egregious or damaging to the organization.

This is a lesson I learned the hard way.

My organization was implementing workflow changes. I supported these changes because they would increase the efficiency of our work. Yet, my manager was resisting these changes.

I didn't bring up my concerns about my manager's resistance with him. Instead, I gossiped and spoke about him to others. I even shared my criticisms of him to the big boss.

I wish I had sat down and talked with my manager one-on-one. Instead, I damaged that relationship.

If you have a concern or issue with your boss, sit down with her and talk about it. Check your assumptions, share your observations, and share your concerns. Focus on actions and behaviors, not on the person.

I did the opposite of lead up. I learned from this experience that preserving a strong relationship and being in partnership with the person I report to is important.

FURTHER LEARNING

Leading Up: How to Lead Your Boss So You Both Win by Michael Useem

Water the Bamboo: Unleashing the Potential of Teams and Individuals by Greg Bell

KEY TAKEAWAYS

- Get clear on expectations and understand your boss's priorities.
- Learn your boss's work styles and communication preferences.
- Communicate well and keep your boss informed of your team's work and progress
- Request guidance and constructive feedback from your boss.
- Create a strong partnership with your boss and support and help them succeed.

COMING UP NEXT: BEGIN YOUR TEAM LEADERSHIP PRACTICE

You've learned the nine team leadership practices covered in this book, and now it's time to begin your journey to becoming a super leader. The next and final chapter instructs you on how you can make a plan to implement these team leadership practices. It also includes a self-assessment so you can see where you are now and create a plan to strengthen your team leadership skills.

BEGIN YOUR TEAM LEADERSHIP PRACTICE

You took time to read this book. You learned nine team leadership practices covered in three parts—lead yourself, lead your team, and lead your boss. Now it's time to begin your team leadership practice and become a super leader.

You can do this! All it takes is time and a commitment to scheduling in time for practicing what you have learned.

This chapter walks through ways you can schedule time in your calendar to put these practices into *practice*. This chapter also includes a self-assessment and steps for creating a six-month improvement plan.

SCHEDULE TIME FOR PRACTICING TEAM LEADERSHIP

The best way to implement these team practices is to schedule time on your calendar. You'll want to schedule:

- Personal time for self-knowledge, reflection, and goal setting

- Planning time
- Uninterrupted, focused work time
- One-on-one time with each member of your team
- Weekly team meetings
- One-on-one time with your boss
- Daily walk around time to interact with your team and your boss

1. Personal time

As you learned in Practice 1, your success depends on doing the work to know yourself better. It's important to know your blind spots, limiting belief, strengths, and weaknesses.

Schedule at least one hour a week of personal time to focus on self-knowledge. Decide the day and time that works best for you. Friday afternoons worked the best for me. I left the office early and headed to my favorite coffee shop. It helped me to get away from the office so I could reflect without distractions on the past week and look at my personal development goals. It was also a nice treat to celebrate my accomplishments from the week.

If you haven't already, use this time to take both the Myers-Briggs assessment (www.mbtionline.com or www.keirsey.com) and *TalentSmart, Inc.*'s emotional intelligence test (www.talentsmart.com).

Also, use this time to develop your leadership purpose. Your leadership purpose defines you, and it will distinguish you as a team leader versus just a supervisor. Create a leadership purpose that inspires you and reflects your values. Download the Leadership Purpose Workbook at https://geni.us/SLbonus and follow the steps.

2. Planning time

Practice 2 gives strategies for working on purpose, including scheduling time for planning.

Schedule a couple hours each week for planning, and a few minutes each day. When you spend time on planning up front, it will make the rest of your time more efficient and effective. That's because you're more likely to work on the things that matter.

During your planning time, identify your priorities and create a to-do list for the week. Your list should include what needs to get done and in what order of priority. As you attend team meetings and take on more assignments, add those to your to-do list and designate the priority. Your list may also include other important yet lower-priority items you can do only if you have time.

Spend a few minutes each day updating your to-do list and looking at your calendar to see what's ahead.

3. Uninterrupted, focused work time

Schedule blocks of uninterrupted, focused work time on your calendar for each day of the week. It is best to schedule four-hour blocks of focused time each day. If four hours is not doable, then schedule two two-hour blocks. Identify and work on your number-one priority during these blocks of time.

If you have flexibility, schedule these blocks of time during the part of the day when you are most productive. Most people are most productive in the morning. Focused work takes mental energy and most of us are more alert in the morning.

4. One-on-one time with each member of your team

The quality of our relationships is integral to everything we do and is the foundation for our success. Having great relationships also makes work more enjoyable and communication easier. Schedule recurring one-on-one meetings with each member of your team. If you have time in your schedule, meet with each person once a week. Otherwise, meet with them at least once a month.

During your one-on-one meetings, strive to get to know your team member better. You can also use these team meetings to coach your team member and clarify expectations.

5. Weekly team meetings

Schedule team meetings that occur at the same time and place each week. These weekly team meetings have many purposes.

First, it gives the team the opportunity to get together and communicate in person. If you have team members who work in different locations, use a video conference service.

Second, weekly team meetings are the best way to hold team members accountable for their assignments and goals. Have each team member report on their progress in meeting their commitments from the prior week. Ask them to share what went well and where they struggled. Also, have each team member share their commitments for the week ahead.

Third, team meetings are great opportunities to practice team building. Team building can include:

- Facilitated team building exercises
- Hot seat sessions where a different team member shares a personal story
- Team name or shared vision discussions
- Feedback practice sessions where team members use example scenarios to practice giving each other feedback

Fourth, it's important to use team meetings to talk about any conflicts or problems. Have the team practice open-minded discussions. Help the team identify issues and dig into them. Help the team explore potential solutions then agree on and implement the solutions. Remind the team of the shared vision and goals and encourage compromise and resolution.

6. One-on-one time with your boss

Your success as a team leader and enjoyment at work will depend on the quality of your relationship with the person you report to. Having a strong relationship with your boss will make communication, resolving conflicts, and receiving feedback easier. Schedule recurring weekly or monthly meetings with your boss. If they are willing, meet them for coffee. Use these meetings to get to know your boss. Also, talk about priorities and how you and your team can align with those priorities.

7. Daily walk-around time

People love being acknowledged and they appreciate when someone asks about them and their life. Go out of your way every day to greet each team member and your boss by name and ask how they're doing. Ask questions about their life outside of work. You can either schedule this time into your calendar or make it a point to acknowledge a different person on your way to a meeting or a trip to the restroom.

SELF-ASSESSMENT: EVALUATE YOUR TEAM LEADERSHIP STRENGTHS AND WEAKNESSES

A key step in developing ourselves is assessing where we are now versus where we want to be. When we learn what skills we need to improve, we can make a plan to improve those skills.

Use this self-assessment to evaluate your team leadership skills. You can download a printable PDF of the Self-Assessment.
https://geni.us/SLbonus

Score yourself for each according to how often you demonstrate the skill:

1 – consistently

2 – sometimes

3 – never

After you score each item, total your score. The first time you take this assessment, your score becomes your baseline. Don't worry about the total number and what it means. No matter your score, there is always room for improvement. Once you have your score, read the section below on how to make a plan for improving your team leadership skills.

TEAM LEADERSHIP SELF-ASSESSMENT

Skill	**Score**

1. I am self-aware and understand my strengths and weaknesses. _____

2. I am proactive in my growth and development and pursue continuous improvement. _____

3. I ask my team members and boss for feedback, and show I can receive feedback well. _____

4. I lead with purpose. _____

5. I work with purpose and implement time management strategies to achieve results. _____

6. I know my team members well and attempt to talk with them often and show I care. _____

7. My team members trust me enough to share their whole selves and to share their concerns and feedback with me. _____

8. I encourage camaraderie, cooperation, and coordination among my team members. _____

9. I foster a safe and positive culture and encourage employees to express their opinions and concerns. _____

10. I encourage and show my team how to have open-minded discussions. _____

11. I delegate by setting clear expectations and providing a high level of support to my team members. ____

12. I give positive, constructive, and timely feedback to team members, and I tie the feedback to a specific expectation or goal. ____

13. When delivering feedback, I express my support and confidence in the person. ____

14. I meet regularly with each team member to help them identify their strengths, weaknesses, dreams, and goals, and to develop an annual plan for how they will improve their skills and reach their goals. ____

15. I coach my team members to help them reach their goals and solve their own problems by asking them questions and listening actively. ____

16. I have made an effort to create a strong relationship and partnership with my boss—we have good rapport and it's easy to be open with my boss. ____

17. I meet with my boss often to confirm expectations and priorities. ____

18. I know my boss's work styles and communication preferences, and I work and communicate well with my boss. ____

Total ____

YOUR SIX-MONTH IMPROVEMENT PLAN

Once you have completed the Team Leadership Self-Assessment, create a six-month improvement plan.

During your scheduled personal time, look at your strengths and weaknesses identified in the assessment and choose three skills you'd like to focus on over the next six months. Why only three? Because you don't want to take on too much at once. If you choose too many things to work on, you might decide you don't have time for any of it.

For each of the three skill areas, pick a goal for each skill that you can reach in six months. When considering goals, ask yourself, *What will it look like to meet this goal?* Next, identify specific actions for how you will improve those skills and reach your goals.

Implement your six-month plan and use your scheduled personal time each week to revisit the plan and to set weekly goals that will help you reach your six-month goals.

After six months, take the self-assessment again to see where you improved. Then, for the next three skill areas you would like to improve in, create a new six-month plan.

READY, SET, GO!

Don't let this be another book you read and put on your shelf (or in your Kindle library) without putting what you learned into practice. Take your success into your own hands. Begin your team leadership practice this week by scheduling your first session of personal time, and then get planning.

I promise if you create a six-month plan and implement that plan, in time you will transform your work life and become a confident team leader—a super leader. You will find yourself with less stress and overwhelm, and you will be able to leave work on time. You will also be able to transform your team into one that thrives and produces exceptional results.

Shanda K. Miller

ACKNOWLEDGEMENTS

This book would not be possible without the guidance and support of the many amazing people in my life. My parents who shaped me to become an independent woman and taught me I could do anything and be anyone if I worked hard enough. My husband, who has given me his unwavering support, including supporting my decision to leave an executive position so I could pursue the dream of writing this book and helping others reach their dreams. All my fellow team members, team leaders, bosses, teachers, and professors, who taught me more than knowledge.

A special thank you to the following individuals for putting your faith in me and supporting this book by pre-ordering copies before I even wrote a single word. Knowing I owed you copies of this book helped keep me motivated. You helped me keep writing even when my limiting belief that "I'm not smart enough" tried to stop me. I kept writing for you, so thank you, and enjoy!

Amy B. Parmenter, MS
Casey Crear, PhD

133

Chelsea D. Clinton, MS, MPA
Harriet Richardson, CPA, CIA, CGAP, CRMA
Jo LeVan, MS
Matthew C. Owens, MBA, CISA
Matt Wessley
Michael J. Barnhart, CPA, CMA, MBA
Michelle Bixler, MPA
Simone D. Rede, CGAP
Stephanie Scafa, MCRP, MPA
Terri Preeg Riggsby, MPA

I also owe many thanks to the staff and community members of Self-Publishing School. After attending a free online workshop and a compelling follow-up call, I joined Self-Publishing School in August 2018. Eight months later I'm ready to publish this book. I can't imagine writing this book without the supportive community of Self-Publishing School. The weekly group coaching calls with Founder Chandler Bolt and Community Manager Sean Sumner were information-packed, my coaching calls with Marcy Pusey were enlightening, my weekly accountability calls with AnnMarie Oh kept me moving forward, and the daily support and encouragement from the Self-Publishing School Community were invaluable. If you too have a dream of writing and publishing a book, make that dream come true and take the first step by signing up for Self-Publishing School's free workshop: https://geni.us/SPS-workshop

REFERENCES

This reference section lists many of the best books and other resources related to the practice of team leadership. I cited information or quotes from these resources and included many of them in the Further Learning sections of each Practice chapter. The references are arranged by chapter and in the order they appear in the book.

PRACTICE 1

Stone, Douglas and Heen, Sheila. *Thanks for the Feedback: The Science and Art of Receiving Feedback Well.* New York: Viking/Penguin Group. 2014.

Drucker, Peter F. *Managing Oneself (Harvard Business Review Classics).* Boston: Harvard Business School Publishing. 2008.

Brown, Brené. *Daring Greatly: How the Courage to Be Vulnerable Transforms the Way We Live, Love, Parent, and Lead.* New York: Gotham Books/ Penguin Group. 2012.

Cain, Susan. *Quiet: The Power of Introverts in a World That Can't Stop Talking*. New York: Crown Publishers/Random House, Inc. 2012.

Website. Myers-Briggs Type Indicator assessment. www.mbtionline.com.

Website. Keirsey. The Four Temperaments. www.keirsey.com.

Bradberry, Travis and Greaves, Jean. *Emotional Intelligence 2.0*. San Diego: TalentSmart, Inc. 2009.

TalentSmart, Inc. *Emotional Intelligence Appraisal* (Results Report for Shanda K. Miller). San Diego: TalentSmart, Inc. 2012.

Website. TalentSmart, Inc. www.talentsmart.com.

PRACTICE 2

Adrain, Lorne A. (Compiled by). *The Most Important Thing I Know: Life Lessons from Colin Powell, Stephen Covey, Maya Angleou and Over 75 Other Eminent Individuals*. New York: Cader Books. 1997.

Wrzesniewski, Amy and Dutton, Jane E. "Crafting a Job: Revisioning Employees as Active Crafters of Their Work." *The Academy of Management Review*. 2001, 26 (2), 179-201.

Wrzesniewski, Amy, Dutton, Jane. E., and Debebe, Gelaye. "Interpersonal sensemaking and the meaning of work." *Research in Organizational Behavior*. 2003, 25, 93–135.

Colman, John. "To Find Meaning in Your Work, Change How You Think About It." *Harvard Business Review*. December 29, 2017.

Sinek, Simon. *Start with Why: How Great Leaders Inspire Everyone to Take Action*. New York: Portfolio/Penguin Group, Inc. 2011

Video file. Sinek, Simon. "Simon Sinek: How great leaders inspire action, 2009." TED: TEDxPuget Sound. 14:02. September 2009. To watch the full talk, visit TED.com.
https://www.ted.com/talks/simon_sinek_how_great_leaders_inspire_action

Keller, Gary and Papasan, Jay. *The One Thing: The Surprisingly Simple Truth Behind Extraordinary Results*. Austin: Bard Press/Rellek Publishing Partners, Ltd. 2012. www.the1thing.com

Morgenstern, Julie. *Never Check E-mail in the Morning: And Other Unexpected Strategies for Making Your Work Life Work*. New York: Fireside/Simon & Schuster, Inc. 2005.

Covey, Stephen R. *The 7 Habits of Highly Effective People: Powerful Lessons in Personal Change*. New York: Free Press/Simon & Shuster, Inc. 2004.

PRACTICE 3

Yaeger, Don. *Great Teams: 16 Things High-Performing Organizations Do Differently*. Nashville: W Publishing/Thomas Nelson. 2016.

Kogon, Kory, Blakemore, Suzette, and Wood, James. *Project Management for the Unofficial Project Manager: A FranklinCovey Title*. Dallas: BenBella Books, Inc. 2015.

PRACTICE 4

Covey, Stephen R. *The 7 Habits of Highly Effective People: Powerful Lessons in Personal Change*. New York: Free Press/Simon & Shuster, Inc. 2004.

Stone, Douglas and Heen, Sheila. *Thanks for the Feedback: The Science and Art of Receiving Feedback Well*. New York: Viking/Penguin Group. 2014.

Morgenstern, Julie. *Never Check E-mail in the Morning: And Other Unexpected Strategies for Making Your Work Life Work*. New York: Fireside/Simon & Schuster, Inc. 2005.

Ventura, Michael. *Applied Empathy: The New Language of Leadership*. New York: Touchstone/Simon & Shuster, Inc. 2018.

PRACTICE 5

Yaeger, Don. *Great Teams: 16 Things High-Performing Organizations Do Differently*. Nashville: W Publishing/Thomas Nelson. 2016.

Tuckman, Bruce W. "Developmental sequence in small groups." *Psychological Bulletin*. 1965, 63 (6), 384–399.

Manges, Kirstin, Scott-Cawiezell, Jill, Ward, Marcia M. "Maximizing Team Performance: The Critical Role of the Nurse Leader." *Nursing Forum*. 2017, 52 (1), 21–29.

Tjosvold, Dean and Tjosvold, Mary. *Building the Team Organization: How to Open Minds, Resolve Conflict, and Ensure Cooperation*. New York: Palgrave Macmillan/St. Martin's Press LLC. 2015.

Gordon, Jon. *The Power of Positive Leadership: How and Why Positive Leaders Transform Teams and Organizations and Change the World*. Hoboken, NJ: Wiley & Sons, Inc. 2017.

PRACTICE 6

Blanchard, Ken and Johnson, Spencer. *The New One Minute Manager*. New York: HarperCollins Publishers. 2015.

Scott, Kim. *Radical Candor: Be a Kick-Ass Boss Without Losing Your Humanity.* New York: St. Martin's Press. 2017.

Stone, Douglas and Heen, Sheila. *Thanks for the Feedback: The Science and Art of Receiving Feedback Well.* New York: Viking/Penguin Group. 2014.

PRACTICE 7

Whitmore, John. *Coaching for Performance: GROWing Human Potential and Purpose – the Principles and Practice of Coaching and Leadership,* 4th Edition. Boston: Nicholas Brealey Publishing. 2009.

Scott, Kim. *Radical Candor: Be a Kick-Ass Boss Without Losing Your Humanity.* New York: St. Martin's Press. 2017.

Stanier, Michael Bungay. *The Coaching Habit: Say Less, Ask More & Change the Way You Lead Forever.* Toronto: Box of Crayons Press. 2016.

PRACTICE 8

Abbajay, Mary. *Managing Up: How to Move up, Win at Work, and Succeed with Any Type of Boss.* Hoboken, NJ: Wiley & Sons, Inc. 2018.

Ballard, John, Ph.D. *Decoding the Workplace: 50 Keys to Understanding People in Organizations.* Santa Barbara: ABC-CLIO, LLC. 2015.

PRACTICE 9

Useem, Michael. *Leading Up: How to Lead Your Boss So You Both Win.* New York: Crown Business/Random House, Inc. 2001.

Abbajay, Mary. *Managing Up: How to Move up, Win at Work, and Succeed with Any Type of Boss.* Hoboken, NJ: Wiley & Sons, Inc. 2018.

Stone, Douglas and Heen, Sheila. *Thanks for the Feedback: The Science and Art of Receiving Feedback Well.* New York: Viking/Penguin Group. 2014.

Bell, Greg. *Water the Bamboo: Unleashing the Potential of Teams and Individuals.* Portland, Oregon: Three Star Publishing. 2009.

ABOUT THE AUTHOR

Shanda K. Miller is a champion for personal and professional development and loves to coach others and help them reach their dreams. Her leadership purpose is to inspire and guide others to live their version of an extraordinary life.

Shanda is living her dream as a leadership coach, trainer, and writer. Shanda seeks to help team leaders break free from stress and lead their teams to high-performance.

She has a Bachelor's Degree in Environmental Science from the University of Idaho, a Master's Degree in Public Administration from the University of Oregon, and 20 years' experience leading teams in the fields of Environmental Science and Performance Auditing.

Shanda spends half her time traveling the world. When not traveling, Shanda and her husband, Kent, live in a tiny house in Eugene, Oregon.

REVIEW REQUEST

Welcome to the World of Super Leaders!

I hope you loved this book! If you did, would you mind leaving an honest review on Amazon?

I would love to hear your thoughts and insights for the book. I welcome your feedback and promise I will receive your feedback well!

Also, please pass this book along to another team leader who may benefit from learning the nine practices of effective team leadership.

Your review and recommendations to friends and colleagues are essential for me to reach a wide audience with this book. This is important because I want to make a difference for team leaders everywhere.

Thank you so much!

https://geni.us/SL-review

TAKE THE NEXT STEP
IN YOUR JOURNEY

Take the next step toward boosting your career and life and improving your team leadership skills.

Book your free 40-minute personalized coaching session with Shanda. During your session, Shanda will work with you to identify your strengths and goals, and your next steps toward becoming a Super Leader.

To learn more about Shanda's training and coaching services, book your free coaching session, or book Shanda for your event, visit shandakmiller.com, email support@shandakmiller.com, or call +1-541-343-0853. Shanda looks forward to working with you!

Made in the USA
Columbia, SC
10 March 2021